children
together

children
together

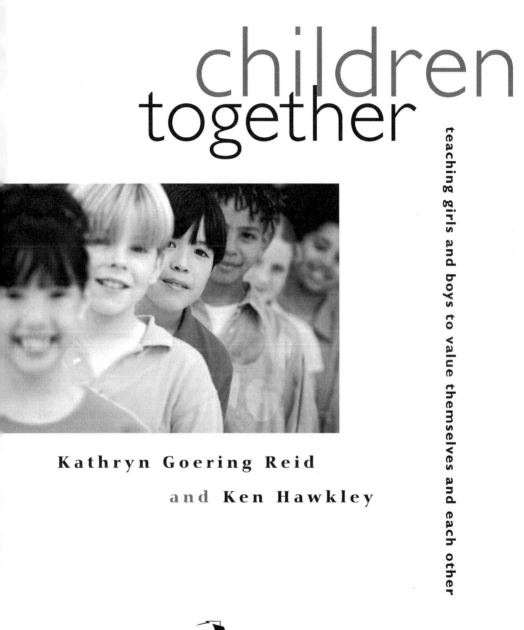

teaching girls and boys to value themselves and each other

Kathryn Goering Reid

and Ken Hawkley

The Pilgrim Press

Cleveland, Ohio

Pilgrim Press, Cleveland, Ohio 44115

Printed in the United States of America on acid-free paper

05   04   03   02   01   00   5   4   3   2   1

Library of Congress Cataloging-in-Publication Data

Reid, Kathryn Goering.
    Children together : teaching girls and boys to value themselves and
each other / Kathryn Goering Reid and Ken Hawkley.
        p.   cm.
    ISBN 0-8298-1380-2 (pbk. : alk. paper)
    1. Self-esteem—Religious aspects—Christianity—Study and teaching
(Elementary).   2. Christian education of children.   I. Hawkley, Ken, 1950–
II. Title.
BV4598.24 .R45   2000
268'.432—dc21

                                                            00-034345

contents

Introduction

Early in life, children learn that color, language, gender, and physical ability differences all too often determine a person's power and capability. They learn this by watching their families, classmates, and others. They see differences and similarities in people they meet, and they observe the reactions of others to these people. The subtle and sometimes not very subtle messages about what to expect from people who are different become very clear.

Listen to children talk about their experiences. In any classroom you can hear comments like these:

"I have to steer the car. I'm a boy. Girls are terrible drivers."

"Don't trust black people. The boys just join gangs. They steal, cheat, and hurt people."

"She's just a baby. She can't even walk. She has to wear crutches."

These messages have a great impact on children. Children grow up believing that differences are more important than similarities. They carry with them hostile and fearful messages that hinder them from forming creative and energizing relationships. They believe that they are superior to some and inferior to others. In the process they lose self-esteem and feel dehumanized.

These messages also have a great impact on our world. Violence is an epidemic in our families. Those who grow up feeling superior begin to believe that it is their right to control and have power over those who are inferior. Many times that power results in battering and abuse.

Unfortunately, too many churches have been reluctant to discuss these inequalities and discrimination. As the violence and abuse continue, we are forced to examine more closely the roots of these problems. We are called to respond by reexamining the messages of God's love for all people and by reading the scriptures that remind us that God empowers all to be God's children.

THE RESPONSE: RELIGIOUS EDUCATION THAT TEACHES EQUALITY

Education within the church and within our families is the only way that the old patterns and habits of discrimination can be overcome. Children are able to learn new attitudes as they become more secure in their identity. Their self-esteem is strengthened, and the entire family can experience the joy of having children and adults, females and males, interacting as whole human beings, empowered by God.

Even though some schools are integrating antibias theory into the classroom, it is essential for the church to become involved in these issues. Our tradition and Scripture clearly mandate that equality is a significant aspect of our Christian faith. Paul reminds us that being part of God's family means leaving racial and ethnic identity, gender, and status in the community behind. Jesus modeled how we can be children of God in his interactions with those who were lowest in the culture, those with disabilities, and those who were looked down upon.

In addition, it is important for the church to no longer allow its institutions or Scripture to be used to make one group of people less valued than others. Persons who wish to justify their superiority frequently misinterpret Scripture or sermons. Therefore, every avenue of communication must be used to spread the gospel message of God's love for all.

PURPOSE OF THIS COURSE

This course has been written to provide kindergartners through eighth graders with an opportunity to appreciate differences among people, to feel more secure in their own identity, and to learn to communicate with and relate to those who are different. All of these discussions are presented in the context of our Christian faith and our scriptural heritage. Many children in middle school have already felt the pain and hurt of discrimination and bias against them.

The purpose of this curriculum is to offer experiences and information on gender issues to be used specifically in churches as part of a religious education program. The ten lessons fit into a typical Sunday morning church school program. However, the material could also be used as curriculum for a special event, perhaps summer vacation church school, an after-school program, or a camping program. The material is written for a broad age group, but is presented in developmentally appropriate levels.

The curriculum draws on excellent secular materials in the field and at the same time relies on biblical materials as the foundation. The curriculum also confronts misinterpretations of biblical materials that have supported discrimination. Through the church's education program, children can learn to reach their own potential and respect the differences in others.

THEOLOGY AND EQUALITY

The Bible contains many stories that reflect the way that God lifted up those who were outcasts from the world culture and society. Ruth was considered inferior because she was from Moab, a land considered evil by the Hebrew people. The man born blind was questioned because the presiding opinion of the time was that a disability was the result of sin.

We have a special perspective on these stories in the Bible. Ruth becomes the ancestor of King David. Jesus models for us acceptance and caring for persons who are different. Jesus' descriptions of the reign of God leave us certain that all people are called to be children of God. Yet we continue to be apprehensive about differences, and we lower a child's self-esteem and potential by stereotyping.

Our religious education programs, established to teach our children our Christian values, reflect our lack of attention to discrimination within our society and our families. All too often Scripture and faith are used to oppress others.

God's message of acceptance and love for all is an empowering message that there is a better way for families to live. Children of all races and abilities can find healthy self-esteem and a strong sense of identity. Girls can learn that they can be competent in all areas and can make choices about their lives. Boys can learn competence without learning to feel and act superior to girls. Children with disabilities can learn alternative abilities, and all children can learn to appreciate those abilities. Everyone can learn to overcome stereotyping. It is our task to teach children that God loves them and that each of us, male or female, is created in God's image.

That is why Bible study, worship, and prayer are essential to each lesson. These disciplines inform our theology that each is a special creation, with God-given abilities and talents. God's love and acceptance are not based on ability, race, gender, economic status, or any other distinction. Our hope is that this curriculum will help children to appreciate the diversity of gifts that boys and girls from all walks of life possess. The heart of this curriculum is to help us communicate, relate, and make peace for all people.

PLANNING FOR THIS COURSE

The curriculum is organized into ten lessons. It is designed for teaching with a compact series of meetings (such as vacation church school) or in consecutive weekly meetings (such as Sunday morning church school). Each lesson is divided into three sections: "Getting Started," "Developing the Lesson," and "Concluding the Lesson." In addition to teaching objectives and a variety of activities, the lessons highlight theological concepts, scriptures, prayers, songs, and other forms of worship experiences for young people.

The curriculum is written for children from kindergarten through eighth grade. Response activities are marked for grade appropriateness. Some response activities are marked with more than one designation because the activity is well suited to a broader range of children.

A unique aspect is the take-home sheet for each lesson. Make enough copies so that each child can have one. The sheet includes a summary of the lesson, discussion questions for the family, a family response activity, parent tips, and information about the next lesson.

The lessons are designed to involve children in the biblical material and the response activities so that they may learn through participation in small group activities and general discussions.

TEACHERS

Even an experienced teacher who agrees to teach these lessons would do well to examine closely his or her teaching style to determine whether gender discrimination is present in the classroom. Many teachers, even unintentionally, have habits and styles that include stereotypes and gender expectations sending subtle messages to children. For example, the physical environment, the frequency of calling on particular children, and the way that follow-up questions are asked can lead some children gradually to believe that they are less capable and less able.

Each lesson includes teaching tips to help teachers look at their styles of teaching and improve their teaching. Habits don't change immediately. However, when a teacher's awareness about bias is raised, new patterns of teaching can emerge.

We recommend a team of two or more people, preferably mixed in gender, to teach the curriculum. This approach allows for flexibility in forming smaller groups. There may be big differences in the maturity, sophistication, and experience of the children.

Although gender issues are important to the way in which all cultures function, some cultural factors can influence the teaching of this material. For example, not all North American native people have the same gender expectations of our broader culture. Therefore, the teacher should be aware of the various cultures represented in the class.

PREPARING THE CHURCH FOR THIS CURRICULUM

Issues of gender, racial and ethnic equality, and discrimination are not often openly discussed in church. Many adults have never had a chance to discuss these issues from the perspective of their faith. Therefore, the teachers need to introduce these topics to both the parents and the entire congregation.

The congregation can be prepared by printing announcements in newsletters and bulletins about the future use of these materials. Some churches find that it is a great opportunity to have an adult education class before or even during these classes. The pastor and other leaders of the church may wish to make public and private affirmations that support the use of these materials. During and after these classes, the leaders of the church may choose to invite the classes to bring materials, role plays, and other activities from the classes to worship. Then the entire church will have a sense of participation in the classes and will have exposure to open discussion about these issues.

STORYTELLING

The stories of the Bible are important elements of the lessons. These methods are used primarily:

- *Acting out first-person dramas.* Ask someone to come to class in costume and to learn the story well enough to tell it to the children. Memorization is not necessary. However, the person in costume must remember the major parts of the story. For this technique, the story has been written out.

* *Telling the biblical story.* As the teacher, read over the story until you can tell it smoothly. Maintain eye contact with the children, and make the story as real as possible. For this technique, the scripture is referenced in the materials.

PARENTS' MEETING

Although most parents appreciate having curriculum that helps their children better understand issues such as gender discrimination and gender equality, some parents have concerns or would like more details about the materials. Before this series of lessons begins, parents and other adults in the church should have an opportunity to look at the materials.

It is strongly recommended that the teachers meet with parents and other interested adults to educate them about the materials. Parents will then be better prepared to respond to the questions and concerns that their children voice. They will also be more prepared to work with their children on the take-home sheet for each lesson. During the parents' meeting, they will have a chance to raise any questions about the content of the course.

SAMPLE PARENT LETTER

Dear Parent,

Family violence and abuse are topics of newspaper articles and television shows, but the roots of violence can be found in issues that are seldom discussed. Discrimination and inequality between people result in mistrust and lack of communication between racial groups and genders. These issues must be discussed in the context of our faith, our churches, and our families.

[*Name of church*] is committed to being a community that cares for children and families. Therefore, we are providing several opportunities for families to learn more about how gender equality and God's love of all can create families with less violence and more communication.

During the next months, [*name of church school class*] will be studying a special church school curriculum on gender equality. We want you to be informed about all aspects of the program. We are providing a Christian educational program that teaches children about God's love for all and gives children tools and understanding to better relate to others.

In addition to the Sunday morning classes for the children, we are offering a workshop on [date] at [time] for parents and other interested adults. This workshop will include information on the lessons themselves.

You are urged to attend this adult workshop. Your questions and concerns could be helpful to us. We hope that you will encourage your child to participate in church school classes during [dates]. If you are unable to attend the adult workshop and you have questions, please feel free to call me.

Sincerely yours,

We Are the Children of God

Biblical Text: Genesis 1:26–31

Focus: This lesson begins our series by focusing on how each person is a special creation of God. By looking at the creation story in Genesis, we are reminded that every person is created in God's image! This is the beginning of our understanding that God created boys and girls as unique individuals. Stereotypes can be very misleading and even hurtful.

Bible Memory: Genesis 1:26–31

Theological/Biblical Perspective

God created all the earth and all the plants and animals. God created man and woman as equals. In Genesis 1:26–31, God's creation is declared good. Human beings are part of creation and also affirmed as being good. All too often, we forget that the goodness of creation includes all human beings. Males and females are created in God's image. This lesson teaches children that they are unique creations of God. They are children of God. In the next lessons, we will look more closely at how each of us relates to others. It is important to realize that loving others begins with loving ourselves.

Anticipated Outcomes

- To increase children's understanding that people, both male and female, are created in God's image.

- To understand that God loves all people.
- To build each child's positive self-image.

Resources Needed

Grades K–2:
- Large sheets of newsprint or a roll of paper
- Markers and crayons

Grades 3–5 and Grades 6–8:
- Envelopes and 3" x 5" cards
- Pencils

All Grades:
- Name tags
- Newspapers
- Scissors
- Masking tape
- Note pads and pencils

Teacher Preparation

1. Read Genesis 1:26–31. Learn the story so that you can tell it with enthusiasm and meaning. Memorizing the story is not necessary; you certainly may use notes. If you don't have time to learn the story, practice reading it so that you can keep the children's interest. (See the note about storytelling in the introduction.)

2. Review the entire lesson.

3. Younger children: Prepare materials for doing the full-size silhouette of each child.

4. Lesson 2 uses photographs of the younger children in the class. You may use an instantly developing camera during the next lesson, or you may want to take regular pictures of all the children in that group during today's lesson in preparation for the next lesson.

5. Learn the theme song (page 8).

GETTING STARTED

Introduce the Course

Begin by introducing yourself. You may know some members of the class and their families through your experience of teaching or your other roles in the church.

Pass out markers and name tags, explaining that we need to be able to call each person by her or his name. Ask each person to introduce herself or himself to the class. If you are new to the group or visitors are present, ask the children to give the class information about themselves. If the class is small, and/or if there are new people or children who are shier than others, invite each child to tell his or her name and favorite color as a way of breaking the ice. If you wish, you may ask them to use their favorite color on their name tags.

Explain that this special time together will show how boys and girls can relate to one another and how we can treat one another more fairly.

Set Ground Rules

Go over your course plans briefly.

Explain that asking questions is helpful to the whole class.

Remind the class that listening carefully to each person is important so that everyone understands what is being said.

Ask students for other class rules to observe. Write them on a large sheet of paper. In the ensuing week, make a poster of these rules to display prominently in the main teaching space.

DEVELOPING THE LESSON: WE ARE PART OF GOD'S CREATION AND GOD'S CREATION IS GOOD

Tell the children about the creation account in Genesis 1:26–31. Highlight some things you heard in this passage. Include the following:

- Human beings are an important part of the creation story.
- Males and females (boys and girls) are made in the image of God.
- God declares that all of the creation, including human beings, is good.
- God created all people of all races and ethnic backgrounds.

All people should be treated with care and respect. Each person—a grown-up or a child—is special.

Remind the class that we are all, male and female, made in the image of God.

Response Activities

Grades K–2 and Grades 3–5: Draw Yourself!

Use butcher paper to draw a full-size silhouette of each child. Ask each child to lie down on the paper, and outline the child's body with a marker. Then encourage each child to draw facial features, hair, clothing, and shoes to make the paper child look like herself or himself.

When everyone is finished, direct the children to look at and talk about what is the same in the drawings and what is different.

Grades 3–5 and Grades 6–8: Give Each Other a Pat on the Back

Tell the class to form a circle. Give each class member an envelope with as many 3" x 5" blank cards as there are people in the class. Ask each person to write his or her name on the envelope.

Begin by asking each person to pass his or her envelope to the person sitting on the right. Next, instruct each person to take out a card and jot down one or more positive things about the person whose name is on the envelope. Then, explain that each of them is to place the card in the envelope and pass it to the next person.

When the envelopes have been all the way around the circle, they should be returned to the owner. Each person will then open the envelope and share with the group the positive things that have been recorded. Some people may choose to add to the list of positive traits. This should be an affirming activity for the class.

All Grades: "In the Image of God"

Note to the Teacher: *This activity is meant as an alternative suitable for all ages.*
Ask the children to form groups of four. Give each group newspaper and masking tape. Encourage them to list some of the ways they think we are made in God's image. What characteristics do we have that God has, for instance: Do we have strength? Are we smart? Are we fast? Then invite them to choose some of these characteristics and fashion something from the newspaper that represents each characteristic. These must be things that the oldest person in the group can wear. Being fast may mean making special shoes; being able to see things may mean fashioning big glasses. After the objects are made and placed on the person, have a fashion show for the others, explaining what each part means.

Introduce the Theme Song "We Are the Children of God" (Appendix)

Give each child a copy of the song "We Are the Children of God."

After singing through the song, discuss the words. Ask, "What does it mean that we are the children of God?"

CONCLUDING THE LESSON

Summarize and Evaluate

Gather the group together for a time to share discoveries made in this lesson. Explain plans for the next lesson.

Closing

Grades K–2: Post around the room the silhouettes that the children made. Ask the class to walk around and look at each picture and say aloud (or silently), "Thank you, God, for [name of child]." Close by singing the song again.

Grades 3–5 and Grades 6–8: Ask the group to form a circle for prayer. Encourage each group member to pray silently for the person who is sitting on the right. Close the prayer with the following words: "Thank you, God, for our parents, our families, and our friends. You made all of us. You made all the boys and all the girls. We remember that each of us is created in your image. Bless us, we pray. Amen!"

✳ TEACHING TIP ✳

Most teachers are unaware of personal biases. Unconsciously, we tend to ask a few children most of the questions or call on the same children. We ask the same children to read orally or to take leadership roles. In recent studies of children in grades 7 and 8, it was discovered that many times girls don't get called on in math.

All children need the attention of the teacher and need the prompting of being asked questions. Don't be embarrassed by your biases, but discover what they are. Ask a friend to observe your teaching, or take your own record. Use a paper listing all the names of the children in your class. Place a mark next to a name each time you call on a child. Mark each time you give a child individual attention.

Look at your results. Do you call on boys more often or on girls? Do specific children receive special attention because they are especially bright or they find church school challenging? Most teachers find that they have a bias. This experiment may give you information about how you can become a better teacher and be more fair with the children in your class. Older children have often been conditioned by teachers so that they respond in class expecting a bias. What a wonderful opportunity you have as a teacher to break down the biases formed by teachers from the past.

PARENT TAKE-HOME SHEET

Lesson 1: We Are the Children of God

In Today's Lesson

We read how God created the world (Gen. 1:26–31).

We discovered that people, both male and female, are created in God's image.

We were reminded that God loves all people.

Family Activity

Why do families spend more time on the negative than on the positive? We argue about differences. We have long discussions about one or two things that we disagree about. All too often we forget to send positive messages.

When we think that each of us is created in the image of God, we are reminded that there is something wonderful and special about each of us. We often take these wonderful characteristics for granted. Today's activity allows us to say things that we often think, but forget to say.

Talking Glasses

Ask all family members to sit in a circle. Find an old pair of sunglasses, and have one family member put on the glasses. The person sitting to the right of the glasses-wearer should say:

Glasses, glasses, say what you see;
Tell what you like best about me!

The person wearing the glasses now talks for the glasses and notes one nice thing about the person who recited the lines.

Pass the glasses to the next person until every family member gets to hear at least one nice thing.

Discussion Questions

- What does it mean that everyone is created in God's image?

- If both males and females are created in God's image, what does God look like?

TO ORDER

{ 1.800.537.3394 }

THE PILGRIM PRESS

THANK YOU FOR YOUR INTEREST IN BOOKS FROM THE PILGRIM PRESS.

Title of book purchased _____

What comments do you have? _____

Why did you purchase this book? (Check all that apply)

❏ Subject ❏ Recommendation of a friend ❏ Information on cover ❏ Gift
❏ Author ❏ Recommendation of reviewer ❏ Appearance of cover ❏ Other ___

If purchased: Bookseller _____ City _____ State ___

I am interested in the following subjects (check all that apply):

❏ African American Resources ❏ General Interest ❏ Religion and Society
❏ Biblical Studies ❏ Justice and Witness ❏ Social Issues
❏ Gay/Lesbian/Bisexual/ ❏ Multicultural/Multiracial ❏ Women's Issues
Transgender ❏ Personal Growth/Spirituality ❏ CURRENT CATALOG

Name _____ Phone _____
Date _____ Fax _____
Address _____ City, State & Zip _____
_____ E-mail address _____

BOOKS AT THE NEXUS OF RELIGION AND CULTURE

THE PILGRIM PRESS

700 Prospect Avenue ■ Cleveland, Ohio 44115
Phone: 1-800-537-3394 ■ Fax: 1-216-736-2206
E-mail: pilgrim@ucc.org ■ Web sites: www.pilgrimpress.com

CALL OUR TOLL-FREE NUMBER, LOG ON TO OUR WEB SITE,
OR VISIT YOUR LOCAL BOOKSTORE.

Information for Parents

Children are creations of God. In their faith development, reminders that God loves them and that each child is created in the image of God are important. Sometimes our society gives children the idea that a particular type of person is loved more than others. For example, God loves one gender more than the other.

Scripture reveals that there are two major commandments. We should love God and love our neighbors. Loving others begins with loving ourselves. Healthy self-esteem can begin with our understanding that God created and loves each one. We can build on our own healthy self-esteem to love others.

Next Lesson

The next lesson will focus on how God loves everyone around the world. We will study how God loves all. No matter what ethnic background or racial identity, each person should be treated with respect and love.

APPENDIX

We Are the Children of God

Lesson Two

Around the World We Are the Children of God

Biblical Text: Ruth 1 (story of Ruth, paraphrased)

Focus: Nations and borders divide people. Skin color and ethnic background contribute to conflict, strife, and war. Young people are often afraid of people with whom they are unfamiliar. Nevertheless, the idea that all people of the world are part of God's family is a concept that children can learn.

Sometimes we forget that God loves those who are different from us. This lesson will focus on how we are called by God to appreciate ethnic and racial differences in people. Around the world and here in North America, children who are Asian, Indian, African American, Native, or Anglo face discrimination. Rather than being uncomfortable with differences, we can learn from our various backgrounds and come to appreciate one another.

Bible Memory: Ruth 1:16–18

Bible Story (told by Ruth, after the birth of her son, Obed)

Would you like to see my young son, Obed? Here he is. I'm so proud of him. He is the only son I have. Boaz, my husband, is also proud of his son. But perhaps the one who is most proud is his grandmother, Naomi. For Naomi, he is her only grandson, and he is a symbol of hope and God's love.

You see, I am not an Israelite. Long ago, there was a terrible famine in this country. Naomi and her husband, Elimelech, came to my home country, Moab, to find work and food. Naomi and Elimelech had two sons. The family must have been desperate and starving to decide to live in Moab because Moabites are hated by the Israelites.

Unfortunately, Elimelech died suddenly. Soon after that, I married one of Naomi's sons. For ten years, we had a happy marriage and good life, but we never had any children. When my husband died, I continued to live with my husband's mother, Naomi. Naomi's other son had also died, and his wife, Orpah, had no children either. At that time, it was especially hard for three women to live together. There was no way for women to make money. We had no way to pay for food, and we were very poor. But I loved my sister-in-law, Orpah, and my mother-in-law, Naomi.

One day Naomi told me that she had decided to return to her homeland. Both Orpah and I told her that we would travel with her. Naomi begged us not to go with her. She knew that Judah would be a difficult place for us Moabite women to live. Although Orpah loved Naomi, she agreed to go back to her parents.

But I pleaded with Naomi to let me go wherever she goes and do whatever she does. I promised to leave my homeland to travel with her. I loved Naomi, my mother-in-law. I knew it would be difficult to be a foreigner in her land.

Even in Naomi's homeland we did not have a way to support ourselves. Life was very hard. I had to go to the fields after the harvest and collect the crop that was missed and dropped. But in the end, things worked out very well. I married Boaz and had this wonderful baby boy.

I want to be sure that you understand that I learned much about Naomi's wonderful God. God loved me, a foreigner. Throughout history, there have been some people who believe that God loves only one group of people, the Hebrew children. Even in the modern world, some people forget that God loves all the people of the earth. God calls all people to be God's children. God loved Naomi. God loves my son, Obed. God loves me, a Moabite woman named Ruth.

Theological/Biblical Perspective

In the biblical story, Ruth is a model of loyalty and support for her mother-in-law. This loyalty takes her on a journey from her own homeland to a place where foreigners, especially foreign wives, were often outcasts. Her homeland, Moab, was considered a land of hostility and evil.

Throughout the world, we continue the prejudice and hatred of past generations. Globally, old tribal strife results in death and destruction for God's children. Nationalism and theories of racial superiority fuel the flames of conflict. We are to remind children that God loves all people. No matter what ethnic background or racial identity, each person should be treated with respect and love. Just as we cannot allow racial and ethnic discrimination to thrive in our world, we cannot permit our children to practice gender discrimination. God loves all people.

Anticipated Outcomes

- To increase appreciation for differences in ethnic backgrounds.
- To understand that God loves all people.
- To learn the story of Ruth.

Resources Needed

All Grades:
- Costume for the character of Ruth

Grades K–2:
- Instantly developing camera or regular photographs taken during Lesson 1
- Brightly colored paper frame for the picture

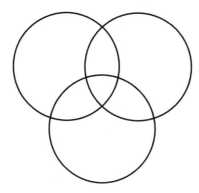

- Large newsprint with three overlapping circles

Grades 3–5:
- Copies of the paper pattern for drawing the people
- Markers or crayons

Grades 6–8:
- Newsprint
- Markers
- Paper and pencils

Teacher Preparation

1. This lesson includes the story of Ruth. This is a wonderful story to be told in first person. Either study the story yourself or ask someone in your church to appear before the class as Ruth after the birth of her son, Obed. Dress in a costume, and hold a life-size doll in blankets. You may even want to encourage the children to ask questions about what happened.

2. (Grades 6–8) Write the unfinished sentences in the response activities on newsprint. If the class is large and will be divided into smaller groups, make more than one copy.

GETTING STARTED

Gather the class together. Explain that for today's lesson, you will have a special guest coming to tell the class about her experience a long time ago. Introduce Ruth to the class. Announce to the group that Ruth was one of the ancestors of Jesus.

DEVELOPING THE LESSON

Ask Ruth to tell her story. (See "Bible Story.")

Lead the class in the appropriate discussion:

Grades K–2: Instruct class members to draw Ruth and Naomi as they arrive in Bethlehem. Ask them to think about what skin color people in Israel would have had. What skin color would Ruth have had? How would she have been treated? Have participants complete their drawings by showing how Naomi and Ruth were welcomed into Naomi's hometown. While they are drawing, ask them some of the questions below. If there is time, invite some children to explain their drawings after they are finished.

- How do you think people treated Ruth, who was a foreigner?
- What are some of the ethnic backgrounds and racial backgrounds in this class?
- Have you ever witnessed or read about someone being treated poorly because of the color of his or her skin?

List the ethnic backgrounds in the class.

List some ethnic/racial backgrounds that are not represented, for example, Asian, Indian, African American, Native, European.

Remind the class that God loves all people.

Grades 3–5: Review the story of Ruth with the class. (See discussion questions with younger children.) Ask the children to plan a welcome party for Naomi and Ruth. What would they do to make Ruth feel welcome? How would they talk to Israelites who hated Moabites? Sometimes people hate other ethnic groups because they are afraid. What could the class do to make people less afraid of Ruth and treat her kindly? If it makes the exercise easier, choose a racial group not represented in the class and plan a welcome party, asking the same questions.

Remind the class that God loves all people.

Grades 6–8: Review the story of Ruth with the class. (See discussion questions with younger children.)

In ancient times, the Hebrew children thought that it was terrible to marry or even talk to a foreigner. Have times changed? If so, how?

List some examples of ways that people of different races and backgrounds are treated unfairly.

Have you ever felt that you were treated unfairly because of your background or race?

What can you do if you see someone treated unfairly?

Response Activities

Grades K–2: Make a Friendly Face

Use an instantly developing camera to take pictures of the children. Help the children glue a paper frame around the pictures. These "Friendly Faces" will be used in the overlapping circle activity.

Overlapping Circles

Draw three overlapping circles on newsprint. The circles should be as large as possible. On one circle, write "yellow." On the others, write "brown" and "black." Invite each group member to put his or her "Friendly Face" on the part of the circle that represents his or her answer. Ask the group members to finish this sentence: "My hair color is . . ."

Show the group how part of the circle represents hair color. The overlapping parts represent someone who has a mixture of two colors. And the very center represents someone who has all three colors in her or his hair.

Grades 3–5: God Loves All the People of the World

Give each child paper patterns to draw people. The children should draw people of different countries, races, and ages. Be sure that both boys and girls are drawn.

After the children finish drawing the pictures, cut out the figures. Make a chain with cutouts of people.

Grades 6–8: Sentence Finishers

Post the following unfinished sentences on the wall. If the class is too large, form smaller groups (three to six people per group).

African women . . .

Japanese men . . .

Mexican women . . .

American Indian men . . .

California girls . . .

Texas boys . . .

Russian girls . . .

English women . . .

American men . . .

African American men . . .

The task of each group is to finish each sentence with as many endings as possible. For example, finished sentences might be "Japanese men are short" and "African American men commit crimes." Give the group about ten minutes to complete this task.

Discuss the responses from each group.

 • Are the ideas expressed facts or ideas that people often have?

 • Are we grouping all people into categories, or do the individuals within these groups vary?

 • How does it feel when your own particular group is mentioned in this way?

 • Are we looking for similarities or differences?

Optional Activity: A Story of Ruth in Our Times

Depending on the size of the class, either form smaller groups or work as a whole. Rewrite the story of Ruth for our time.

Remember Ruth was a Moabite. The Hebrew people hated her people. What people are disliked in your community? Would Ruth be Hispanic, African American, or Russian? Could Naomi be from Bosnia and Ruth from Serbia? Is Naomi from white South Africa and Ruth from black South Africa?

Write the story so that it is similar to the biblical story, but use modern ethnic and racial groups to update it.

Ask each group to read its version. Discuss the different versions that the class created.

CONCLUDING THE LESSON

Summarize and Evaluate

Gather the class together and ask participants to share ideas and feelings about what happened in the lesson. Explain the plans for the next lesson.

Closing

Remind the class that God loves everyone. Read aloud Galatians 3:28. Ask participants to name places in the world where people don't get along. Don't forget people here in North America that are uncomfortable with one another. Pray that the world will find peace and will better understand people who are different.

✳ TEACHING TIP ✳

Many adults are afraid to bring up issues such as prejudice and discrimination because they believe that children's lives are unaffected by these issues. They are afraid that perhaps they will force children to face adult situations too early or shatter their early childhood innocence.

However, research data challenge these assumptions:

- Studies have shown that children begin to notice differences and construct categories of differences in people very early.

- Children's identity and attitudes are rooted in their own developmental tasks and steps.

- Stereotyping and bias influence children's self-esteem and attitudes toward others.

Therefore, it is important to talk about these difficult issues. Children at an early age already see unfair things happening around them. They are already accepting and adjusting their worldview by the way they are treated and the way they see others being treated in the world.

A teacher should not be afraid to allow children to express their feelings. Even young children often have stories to tell about times when someone experienced discrimination. Although they might not use grown-up terms and words for their experience, they understand hostility and hatred all too well. We must encourage our children to have strong identities and respect others who are different. We can do that only when we confront racism in our world.

PARENT TAKE-HOME SHEET

Lesson 2: Around the World We Are the Children of God

In Today's Lesson

We learned about the story of Ruth, a Moabite woman who became the ancestor of Jesus.

We are learning to appreciate the differences in the ethnic backgrounds of people in the world.

We were reminded that God loves all the people of the world.

Discussion Questions

- Do you know people from a different ethnic background?
- Where do they come from?
- Where do your ancestors come from?
- What are some of the differences and similarities between your family and their families? (Note things such as celebrations, foods, customs, dress, attitudes, etc.)

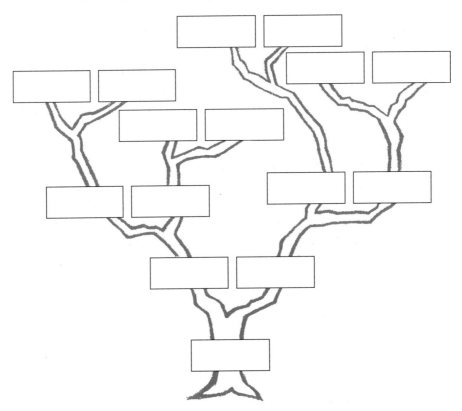

Family Activity

Fill in the family tree. Under the name of each family member, write his or her country or ethnic background. After you fill out the family tree together, think about how different the family tree might be for some of your neighbors or friends.

Information for Parents

Children are often sensitive to the feelings of their parents. Perhaps it is natural that both adults and children feel uncomfortable or anxious when they encounter something new. When we meet someone from another culture or ethnic background, we may feel uncertain. It is important that we give our children opportunities to meet others who are different and that we encourage our children to appreciate these differences.

Plan an experience for your family in which you can encounter another culture. Ask a Jewish family if you can celebrate Passover or Sabbath with them. Go to an ethnic church to worship on a Sunday morning. Travel to an American Indian special event. Ask a family from another country to share some experiences that show differences and similarities.

Next Lesson

We will be learning about God's love for the special gifts of people who are differently abled. God loves everyone. There are many ways that people are different. Some of us have special talents and gifts.

Special People Are the Children of God

Biblical Text: John 9:1–3 (the story of the man born blind)
Focus: For centuries, people believed that God was punishing persons with disabilities. Jesus gave us a different model. Particularly in the story about the man born blind, Jesus reminded those around him that the man was not blind because he or his parents were being punished.

Overcoming the prejudices in our culture means teaching children to appreciate the gifts of children with special needs—visual, mental, developmental, and physical challenges. This lesson reminds us that everyone has been given special gifts and talents.
Bible Memory: Galatians 3:26–29

Theological/Biblical Perspective

We know that each person is unique and God loves each person, but we may overlook the gifts of children with special needs. As our society focuses more and more on the perfect young image portrayed in the media, anyone who does not fit that image can be seen as an outsider and an alien. This lesson reminds us that not only does God call us to treat everyone with respect and dignity, but God also calls us to appreciate the gifts of each person. No matter what a person's ability, it is a gift from God. We are once again reminded that God loves each one of us.

Anticipated Outcomes

- To understand that God loves each person, regardless of a person's abilities or disabilities.
- To increase our appreciation of the gifts of children with special needs.
- To identify the variety of gifts that God has given us.

Resources Needed

Grades K–2 and Grades 3–5:
- Rubber ball
- Various items to allow the children to experience disabilities: blindfolds, earplugs, wheelchairs, walkers, crutches, etc.

Teacher Preparation

1. Look over the introductory sketch. Particularly in a small church where everyone is known, it is important for this sketch to reflect reality. In the blanks, use real talents of the adults to illustrate the point that everyone has talents. Think of talents such as playing an instrument, making a craft, singing, having a sense of humor, writing a poem, being a good friend, or any others.

2. Review the entire lesson.

3. Have copies of the theme song to use in the closing.

GETTING STARTED

For the opening sketch, one adult should set up and begin to do some kind of enjoyable activity or hobby. The other adult shows curiosity about that talent or gift.

FIRST ADULT: Today we are going to look at special gifts of each person. I'm going to share my hobby with you.

SECOND ADULT: Hey, what's all this stuff?

FIRST ADULT: I thought that I would share my talent with the class. So I brought all this stuff to show the class.

Second Adult: That's great. You really do have a talent.

First Adult: Well, it is something that I really enjoy, and I'm good at this.

Second Adult: Tell us a little bit about your talent.

First Adult: [*Tells about the talent or hobby.*]

Second Adult: Wow! This is great. I wish I had a talent like that. Look at what you can do. God blessed you with a great talent.

First Adult: I think God gave each of us a talent. However, I can't do everything. No one can.

Second Adult: Well, God probably gave most of us a talent, but I'm not sure that I have one.

First Adult: Of course you have talents. Let's see. I know that you have a talent for _____. You are really good at that.

Second Adult: I never thought of that as a talent. I'm also good at _____. That's really a talent.

First Adult: Everyone has a talent if he or she just thinks about it. Sometimes it takes friends to remind us what our talents really are. We must also realize that there are things we can do that others can't.

Second Adult: And things others can do that we can't.

First Adult: Right! God has given each of us a unique set of gifts and abilities. We are all differently abled!

DEVELOPING THE LESSON

Make a list of talents and gifts.

Use newsprint to make a list of talents. Start with the talents named in the sketch.

Review the list:

- ◆ Do some talents need training?
- ◆ Are there some talents that older people are better at than others?
- ◆ Are there some talents that younger people are better at than others?
- ◆ Are some talents only for boys or girls?
- ◆ Are some talents for only one racial or ethnic group?
- ◆ Are some talents harder for someone who is disabled?

✳ TEACHING TIP ✳

In our society we often have stereotypes about what kinds of talents people have. We think that African Americans are better basketball players and dancers. Asian Americans are smarter than other people. People of European descent are often thought to be good at classical music. Men are better athletes and drivers. Women are better at schoolwork. People in wheelchairs can't participate in sports.

We may fail to recognize the talents of people because they don't fit into our stereotypes of what people really can do. As the class reviews the talents, it is important that these stereotypes are broken. Point out that anyone can have these talents. Each person has a talent. Be sure to affirm everyone's talents.

Bible Story

Ask the class to name some disabilities, for example, blindness or visual impairment; deafness or hearing impairment; developmental delays; brain damage; paraplegia; dyslexia and learning differences.

Ask the children if they know anyone who is disabled.

Remind the class that the Bible story today is about a man who was born blind. When someone is disabled, we often want to know what caused the disability. Sometimes doctors can tell us why a person is born unable to hear or to see.

Read John 9:1–3. Point out to the class how the disciples wondered whether the blindness was caused by sin. The disciples thought that perhaps the man or his parents had committed some terrible act. They thought that God would punish people by making the man blind at birth.

Jesus answered the disciples by saying that the blindness had nothing to do with sin. Jesus said that the man was born blind to show God's power.

Reinforce the idea that disabilities are not caused by someone's sin. Many times doctors don't have any idea about why a baby might be disabled. Sometimes people are disabled because they were in an accident or they were ill.

Optional Activity

Invite someone with a disability to visit the class. Although the children will have questions about how the guest became disabled, try to focus the class on the talents and gifts of the person. For example, someone in a wheelchair can play sports. Someone who is blind can play an instrument.

Encourage the person to tell how the disability in one obvious area has helped in other areas. For instance, people who are blind often develop other senses that are more acute.

Remind the class that everyone has strengths and weakness. Each of us can't do some things, but we are very talented in other things.

Response Activities

Grades K–2 and Grades 3–5: Talents Game

Direct the class to sit in a circle. Pick up a rubber ball, and throw it to one person in the circle. As the person catches the ball, he or she must name one talent that he or she has. Then that person throws the ball to another person who has not yet been picked.

When the ball has been passed to each class member, give everyone another turn.

Remind the class that each person has talents and everyone can be proud of the talents in a way that is not bragging. Explain that having gifts that are different from others is a sign of being one of God's unique creations.

Grades K–2 and Grades 3–5: Experience a Disability

Encourage the class to try different disabilities. Provide blindfolds so that some students can imagine what it is like to be blind. Use earplugs so that some can experience what it is like to be hearing impaired. Borrow a wheelchair so that children can experience trying to move around the room with a wheelchair.

Remind the class that even though it might be fun to try these experiments, it would be more difficult to continue them for an extended period of time.

✳ TEACHING TIP ✳

Role playing is an excellent way to learn skills. Use the role playing as an opportunity for the group to learn how to handle difficult situations in a safe environment.

- Introduce the activity as "pretending." This pretending is skill practicing.
- Do not comment on the child's performance as an actor. Any evaluation should concern the child's use of information and skills.

* Give lots of positive reinforcement. Acting and answering questions about role playing can be frightening, and children may need extra encouragement and reinforcement that they are doing fine.

* *Use only volunteers for role playing.* Some children are not comfortable playing a role. They learn best by watching others.

* Always talk about the role play afterward. Give the children an opportunity to express what they felt during the role play.

Grades 6–8: Role Play

1. Read the following background story: "Jesse and his friend Juanita missed the bus from school. They are both middle school students in the seventh grade. After calling his mother, Jesse waits with Juanita near the bus stop for his mother to pick him up. Other students are also waiting for rides. One of the students is mentally disabled. Several students, both boys and girls, start picking on the student. They call him names, such as 'moron' and 'dummy.'"

2. Ask the class to brainstorm about what Jesse and Juanita do. Then invite some students to act out the solution. If solutions are not presented, here are options to suggest to the class. Do not offer these too quickly; the students will learn more by thinking out their own solutions.

a) One option might be to say something to the other students. As the teacher in the class, pretend that you are one of those students who is picking on the disabled student. Ask two students to be Jesse and Juanita. What can they say to the other students?

b) Another possible action would be to talk to an adult in the school—a teacher, administrator, or counselor. What should they say to this adult? Ask two students to be Jesse and Juanita while the teacher pretends to be the adult they talk to.

Another Role Play

1. Read the following background story: "Veronica and Scott are walking home from church on a Sunday. They meet a woman in a wheelchair trying to cross the street. The cars are driving very fast. They worry that the woman might not be safe."

2. What should they do? Ask the class for two volunteers to play the parts of Veronica and Scott. The teacher can be the person in the wheelchair.

Note: Explain to the class that it is important to ask a disabled person how you can help. Children should not be afraid to talk to the person, but always ask before assuming that they should help. It might be a good idea to have the person in the wheelchair want help one time and another time refuse help.

✳ TEACHING TIP ✳

After demonstrations, role playing, or other forms of participation, the teacher should affirm persons and ideas. The affirmation can be for either the individual or the whole group. Some examples include: "Some good ways and ideas shared today were . . . ," or "Thank you for sharing . . ."

CONCLUDING THE LESSON

Summarize and Evaluate

Direct the group to form a circle. Encourage the class to think about this lesson. Answer any questions from the class, and reinforce the ideas in this lesson. Explain the plans for the next lesson.

Closing

Group prayer: Ask each person to think of one gift or talent that he or she can name. Invite each one to finish this sentence: "One of my gifts is that I can . . ." After each person names his or her talent, encourage the class to say, "Thank you, God, for your many gifts!"

Remind the class that prayers do not have to be all quiet and silence. Suggest that the class say with enthusiasm, "Thank you, God, for your many gifts!"

Sing the theme song "We Are the Children of God."

PARENT TAKE-HOME SHEET

Lesson 3: Special People Are the Children of God

In Today's Lesson

We were reminded that God loves each person, regardless of a person's abilities or disabilities.

We learned to better appreciate the gifts of children with special needs.

We learned to identify the variety of gifts that God has given us.

I learned to say some positive things about myself without bragging.

Discussion Questions

- Does your family know anyone who is disabled?

- Are there any family members who have disabilities?

Review that God loves every human being.

Family Activity

For the next week, all family members will keep track of the loving actions they do for one another. Each person will write a note about each loving action and put the note into a box called "God's Loving Family Box."

As a family, decorate a box (shoe box size) with symbols of our faith. Crosses, lilies, and butterflies are symbols of resurrection. Rainbows are the symbol of God's promised care. The lamb is a symbol of Christ. Label the box "God's Loving Family Box." Cut a 1" x 6" slot in the top of the box. On the bottom of the box cut out a small 4" x 4" door. Use masking tape to close the door on the bottom of the box.

Put the box in the center of the table with pencils and 3" x 5" cards.

Begin this activity by gathering family members and reviewing what loving actions might be. Ask each person to name one example of a loving action. Point out that whenever a family member does one of these actions, he or she should describe that action on a card and put it into the box. Children who are too young to write may draw a picture of the loving action or dictate it to someone older.

At the end of the day (or at dinnertime), gather the family together and open the door on the bottom of the box. Remove the cards and read each card aloud. End this family time with a simple prayer thanking God for each person in this family.

Parent Tip

Negative feelings and discomfort around others who are different often come from our own insecure and negative feelings about ourselves. Children who feel good about themselves have more confidence in their interactions with others.

Children can understand that all children, even disabled children, are part of God's creation. Every human being has gifts and graces that are wonderful. Each contributes to our world.

Next Lesson

The next lesson will focus on how girls and boys are different and how they are the same. Just as we must overcome our stereotypes and misunderstanding of disabled people, we must overcome misunderstanding of gender differences.

What Do Girls Do?
What Do Boys Do?

Biblical Texts:

Genesis 25:27–30, 34: Jacob cooks a meal; Esau is a hunter.

Judges 4:1–8: Deborah is a ruler and judge.

1 Samuel 16:15–23: David plays the harp.

Luke 10:38–42: Mary is a student and Martha is a homemaker.

Acts 16:13–15, 40: Lydia is a businesswoman and church leader and founder.

Focus: During this lesson, we want to help children recognize gender stereotypes. Often we assume that men and women are limited to certain tasks and responsibilities based on their gender rather than on their gifts and abilities. This lesson will help children examine these types of assumptions and begin to look beyond stereotypes to the real person.

Bible Memory: 1 Corinthians 7:7b

Theological/Biblical Perspective

Throughout the biblical text, men and women are described in various roles. Both men and women were in leadership roles in the Old Testament (Deborah and Samuel were judges) and in the New Testament (Lydia and Timothy were church leaders).

Although we often think of serving others as women's work, both men and women are portrayed in serving roles. For example, Jacob cooked, David served Saul, and Martha served Jesus.

God realizes the potential in every person. Women can be leaders. Men can be servers. In both Old and New Testaments, we see examples of people using their gifts in a variety of ways.

Anticipated Outcomes

• To understand that the Bible describes nontraditional gender roles such as women in leadership positions and men in serving positions.

• To increase the understanding of the children that gender should not limit their own interests and activities.

• To share feelings and assumptions about traditional role limits.

Resources Needed

Grades K–2:

•"Our Friendly Faces" (the circle with a picture of each class member) from lesson 2

• Tape

• A photocopy of "Whose Toys Are These?" (Appendix 4B) for each child

Grades 3–5 and Grades 6–8:

• Materials for making a book: construction paper for cover, glue, white paper, hole punch, and string to tie it together

Grades 3–5:

• A photocopied sheet of "Whose Toys Are These?" (Appendix 4B) for each child

• Newsprint and markers, or chalkboard and chalk

Grades 6–8:

• Newsprint and markers, or chalkboard and chalk

• An overhead projector and overhead of Appendix 4C

• Paper and pencils

Teacher Preparation

1. Prepare the opening teacher skit (Appendix 4A).

2. Prepare for the activities and discussion that will introduce the theme for this week. See the three suggested activities.

3. For younger children, prepare the pages for creating the book "What Can Girls Do? What Can Boys Do?" Write the lines for the first pages using the biblical figures studied in the Bible lesson.

❋ TEACHING TIP ❋

During any discussion, it is important to ask follow-up questions. The first response of a child may be the correct answer, but a child needs to develop critical thinking skills. For example, when a group member suggests that both boys and girls enjoy many activities, the teacher should follow up that answer by asking, "Why do you think that?" or "What activities do you enjoy that a person of the other sex might enjoy too?" Asking follow-up questions of group members encourages the group to reason and think about the answers.

However, teachers should ask all group members follow-up questions. Recent studies report that many teachers show a preference in asking only boys follow-up questions. Teachers should encourage analytical and critical thinking skills in children of both sexes.

4. For the children in the middle grades, make copies of the pictures for the "Whose Toys Are These?" exercise on page 41. Perhaps they can cut out the circles, or you may want to do that beforehand.

5. For the young people in junior high, make sure you have enough copies of the continuum exercise for each member. Provide masking tape to set up a larger version on which to compile all the results from the exercise.

6. Learn the song for today's lesson.

GETTING STARTED

1. Welcome class members and begin the teacher skit. (See Appendix 4A.)

2. Introduce the lesson theme. These activities are meant to prepare the students for the upcoming discussion. You may refer to the results from these activities later in the lesson.

DEVELOPING THE LESSON

Grades K–2: Overlapping Circles

Draw three overlapping circles on newsprint. On one circle, write "sports." On the others, write "playing housekeeping" and "riding a bike."

Ask each group member to put his or her "Friendly Face" (created in lesson 2) on the space that matches the activity they like to do best. If they like two of the activities, their "Friendly Face" goes into the appropriate overlap area. If they like all three activities, their "Friendly Face" goes in the center space. The group members are then invited to finish the sentence "I like . . . ," listing the activities they like to do.

Show the students how part of the circle represents that they like to do only one of the activities. The overlapping parts represent someone who likes to do two activities. The very center represents someone who likes to do all three activities. The class will be familiar with this activity because the class will be doing these overlapping circles several times during this series of lessons.

Review the group's answers:

+ Who liked to ride bikes? Who liked to play housekeeping? Who liked sports?
+ Which activity did more boys like?
+ Which activity did more girls like?
+ Is there a reason girls might like one activity or another?
+ Are these activities that all children might enjoy?
+ Are these activities that teach children important skills? For example, both boys and girls need to learn how to be good parents, and playing with dolls is part of practicing.

Whose Toys Are These?

Using the circles with pictures of toys (Appendix 4B), give each child a photocopied sheet. Instruct them to cut out all the circles. Tape three large sheets of construction paper or newsprint on the wall, side by side. One should be titled "Boys," one should be titled "Girls," and the middle one should be titled "Boys and Girls." Ask the children to decide which toys belong on which sheet. Provide tape, and allow them to attach their pictures to the proper sheet. (These sheets could be on different walls.)

For discussion: What makes a toy a girl's toy or a boy's toy? Which of these toys would you like to play with?

Grades 3–5 and Grades 6–8: Identify Gender-based Activities

On a sheet of newsprint or on a chalkboard, make two columns labeled "Girls" and "Boys." Ask group members to list activities that girls do in one column and activities that boys do in another. For example, in the column under "Girls," the group might list sewing, bike riding, playing volleyball, being a member of the band. In the column under "Boys," the group might list playing football, watching television, being a member of the band. Make the list as long as possible.

Analyze the list. Ask the group the following questions:

- What activities are listed on both lists? On only one list? Why?

- Are there any activities that you might enjoy that others might think are inappropriate for your gender?

- Are there career choices that are for only one gender: a doctor, a nurse, a minister, a police officer, president?

- Is it right to keep someone from a career because of his or her gender?

Remind the group that many times our society labels certain activities and careers for one gender or another, but it doesn't have to be that way.

Biblical Texts

Genesis 25:27–30, 34: Jacob cooks a meal; Esau is a hunter.

Judges 4:1–8: Deborah is a ruler and judge.

1 Samuel 16:15–23: David plays the harp.

Luke 10:38–42: Mary is a student and Martha is a homemaker.

Acts 16:13–15, 40: Lydia is a businesswoman and church leader and founder.

(Note to the teacher: *Cover this opening paragraph with the class and then read or ask someone else to read the biblical texts or read them as stories. Two examples are given.*)

Some people think that boys or men should do only certain activities and women or girls should do only certain other activities. Sometimes there are good reasons for thinking this way, but many times there are no good reasons. For instance, many people regard cooking as a task meant for women. The Bible, though, describes men and women doing things because of their gifts and abilities, not because of their gender.

When the boys grew up, Esau was a skillful hunter, a man of the field, while Jacob was a quiet man, living in tents. Isaac loved Esau, because he was fond of game; but Rebekah loved Jacob. Once when Jacob was cooking a stew, Esau came in from the field, and he was famished. Esau said to Jacob, "Let me eat some of that red stuff, for I am famished!" . . . Then Jacob gave Esau bread and lentil stew, and he ate and drank, and rose and went his way. (Gen. 25:27–30, 34)

At that time Deborah, a prophetess, wife of Lappidoth, was judging Israel. She used to sit under the palm tree of Deborah between Ramah and Bethel in the hill country of Ephraim; and the Israelites came up to her for judgment. She sent and summoned Barak son of Abinoam from Kedesh in Naphtali, and said to him, "The God of Israel commands you, 'Go, take position at Mount Tabor, bringing ten thousand from the tribe of Naphtali and the tribe of Zebulun. I will draw out Sisera, the general of Jabin's army, to meet you by the Wadi Kishon with his chariots and his troops; and I will give him into your hand.'" Barak said to her, "If you will go with me, I will go; but if you will not go with me, I will not go." (Judg. 4:4–8)

Reflect on the Bible passages: Who is doing what? What role is different? Learn the song "Who Is a Disciple?" (Appendix 4D). It will be a good song to repeat during other lessons in this series.

Response Activities

Grades K–2 and Grades 3–5: Create a Book

Show the class the title page of the book "What Can Girls Do? What Can Boys Do?" Also show them the pages that already have this text:

Some people say that only men can be judges and government leaders, but Deborah was a judge and a leader in the Bible and she was a woman.

Some people say that only women can be poets, but David was a poet in the Bible and he was a man.

Some people say that only women can cook, but Jacob made stew in the Bible and he was a man.

Brainstorm about what to put on the other pages using the same pattern: "Some people say that only boys can [*activity name*], but [*girl in the class*] can [*activity name*] and she's a girl." Use real examples from the group's experience. The teacher can write these lines on additional white pages.

Encourage each group member to select a page to illustrate. After the illustrations have been made, punch holes and string the book together.

Gather the group together to read the book. Review the basic ideas of this lesson with the class:

- What can girls do?

- What can boys do?

Emphasize that all group members have talents, and God wants each person to use his or her talents.

Grades 3–5: What Do You Like to Do?

Ask the group members to complete Appendix 4E. Then ask these questions:

- Can you give reasons why you like or dislike the activities on the list?

- Are there some activities that you think boys would like more than girls would? Which ones?

- Are there some activities that you think girls would like more than boys would? Which ones?

- Are there some activities on the list you have done at least once but don't do anymore?

- Are there activities on the list that you would like to try?

Grades 6–8: Masculine or Feminine?

This exercise may be used with an overhead if one is available, or the leader may do it verbally. Give each member a blank sheet of paper, and explain that the class is to make a column of numbers from 1 through 10 on the left-hand side of the page. Use the sheet provided (Appendix 4E) to make an overhead or to be used verbally. It will not work well if given as a written assignment. If you use an overhead projector, cover the words so that they are revealed one at a time. Allow no more than five seconds for a response. You want spontaneous reactions so as to be able to discuss stereotypes that we learn constantly in unconscious ways.

You could say something like this before beginning the exercise: "Look at these ten words one at a time. Be sensitive to your first reaction to these words. Do not think about them; simply put down your first reaction. If you think any of these words pertain to a female, put an 'f' beside the number. If you think the word pertains to a male, put an 'm' beside the number. Don't go back and think about it."

After the exercise, ask for a show of hands indicating who put down what for each of the words. Ask the students why they made the choices they did:

- Would you have made the same choices if you had had more time to think?

- What do the choices tell us about our attitudes and assumptions about gender?

- Where do you think you learn these assumptions?

- Should we try to change the assumptions indicated by this exercise? If so, how? If not, why?

CONCLUDING THE LESSON

Summarize and Evaluate

Spend a few minutes recalling what has happened during this lesson.

Closing

Answer any questions from the group about the topics in today's lesson, and sing the song that the class learned today.

Ask the group either to stand or to sit in a circle while you pray the following reflective prayer. "Wonderful, wise Creator, you made each of us. You made some of us boys and some of us girls. You gave each of us talents and gifts. Help us to use our talents to make the world a better place for all of your children. Amen."

PARENT TAKE-HOME SHEET

Lesson 4: What Do Girls Do? What Do Boys Do?

In Today's Lesson

We explored perceptions about activities and tasks that girls and boys like to do.

We discussed the similarities and differences in the interests of both boys and girls.

We discovered that some of our assumptions are neither fair nor accurate.

We discovered that the Bible portrays men and women in roles considered nontraditional. For example, Deborah was a judge and tribal leader (Judg. 4:1–8), Jacob cooked (Gen. 25:27–30, 34), and David wrote poetry (1 Sam. 16:15–23).

Family Activity

List family tasks (washing dishes, doing laundry or yard work, etc.). Then use these discussion questions for parents and kids:

- Which tasks or responsibilities do family members have?
- Who assigns the tasks?
- Who else might be able to do these tasks?
- What tasks do you enjoy learning about?
- Would another system of assigning tasks be fairer to all members of a family?

Everyone Working Together

This table can be used to look at who does what tasks around the house and how the tasks can be shared more equitably. All adults and children in the house are encouraged to participate. Name a household task and write that in column 1. In the next column, list the person who is usually responsible for that activity. In the last column, discuss who might be able to do it so that everyone takes responsibility for tasks. This is an opportunity to give children important responsibilities, not simply for an adult to shift unpleasant activities. Children love a challenge and take pride in a job well done, especially when it is acknowledged.

Household Activity	Who Usually Does It?	Who Else Can Do It?

Parent Tip

In our modern world, families choose different roles for different people. Often children think of the roles as rigid and nonchanging. For example in some families, one parent always does the laundry and children take out the garbage.

Families that have more flexible roles find that children increase their self-esteem and self-worth by becoming adept at a variety of tasks. Sharing task assignments and rotating jobs allow family members to explore their potential. It is important that parents encourage children to explore nontraditional tasks. For example, girls can help fix mechanical devices, and boys can cook. All of these tasks help children learn to be independent and self-confident. In addition, these tasks help children appreciate the work that parents do and build the understanding that families need to work together.

Next Lesson

The topic is "Exploring Our Potential: Look What I Can Do!"

APPENDIX 4A

Practice this dialogue with the other teacher or helper in the class. The best combination would be for a woman to play #1 and a man to play #2. This is a simple and light way to introduce some very serious subjects. Using a light tone in the skit may open up discussion later on. There should be no preliminary introduction; begin with this dialogue.

1: Well now, I'd like to introduce our lesson today

2: Wait a minute. I thought I was going to introduce the lesson.

1: No, I think I should do it.

2: I spent a lot of time preparing.

1: Oh, and you think I didn't?

2: Well, I should do it anyway because I'm the man.

1: But I'm the woman.

2: Men are stronger.

1: Women are smarter.

2: Men are better speakers.

1: Women are more organized.

2: Men talk louder.

1: Women talk faster.

2: My introduction is better.

1: How do you know?

2: Well . . . it just is.

1: Why don't we compare?

2: Okay. I was going to tell the class that we were going to look at some of the things that we say only boys can do or only girls can do.

1: I was also going to tell them that and add that when we say only boys or girls can do something, that is called an assumption. When our assumptions are not true, we stereotype people. That is not fair.

2: It's not fair because there are things that boys do that girls like to do. And there are things that girls do that boys like to do.

1: We should get to know our friends as people who have different gifts and talents. Though girls and boys are different, that is often not a good reason to think that a person will not be good at doing something.

2: Right, boys and girls like to do lots of things, and they should be allowed to find out the things they are interested in or are good at without worrying whether it is a "girl thing" or a "boy thing."

1: Say, we did pretty well.

2: Yes, working together was fun.

APPENDIX 4B

Whose Toys Are These?

Have each child cut out the circles. Invite each child to divide the pictures into three piles: one pile for toys that are only for girls, another pile for toys that are only for boys, and a third pile for toys that are for either girls or boys.

APPENDIX 4C

Make a transparency from this sheet.
Masculine or Feminine?

1   Seduce

2   Virgin

3   Leader

4   Doctor

5   Teacher

6   Nurture

7   Curved

8   Angled

9   Talkative

10   Intelligent

APPENDIX 4D

Who Is A Disciple?

Words and music by Jean Strathdee. Copyright © 1991 by Desert Flower Music, P.O. Box 1476, Carmichael CA 95609. Used by permission.

APPENDIX 4E

Below is a thick line with the numbers 1 through 5 underneath it. Below that line is a list of activities that children your age like to do. Beside each activity is a letter of the alphabet. Look at each activity and the corresponding letter, indicating whether you like or dislike that activity. Not everyone likes all of the activities listed. That's okay.

If you like bicycle riding very much, put the letter "a" close to the end of the bar that says "like." If you like doing it a little, put your letter near the middle of the line (close to the number 3). If you like an activity a lot, put your letter closer to the "like" end of the line (closer to number 5). If you don't like it, place your letter closer to the "dislike" end of the line.

dislike				like
1	2	3	4	5

a. riding a bicycle

b. skipping rope

c. playing with dolls

d. playing with Legos

e. reading

f. writing

g. writing stories

h. playing sports

i. building model rockets

j. playing computer games

Exploring Our Potential: Look What I Can Do!

Bible Text: John 4:7–42; 1 Corinthians 12:17–25 (many gifts)

Focus: In this lesson, we want to let children see what men and women can do that breaks traditional stereotypes. We also want to let the children discover and talk about some of the things they can do.

When we look at the world around us, as well as the church of which we are a part, what do we see that teaches children about gender stereotypes? Whether the situations are intentional or not, there are many limitations that we support actively or that we support through our inactive confrontation of minor injustices.

The biblical emphasis in this lesson is on Jesus' view of the potential in a person who was not highly regarded. First of all, she was a woman. Second, she was a Samaritan. Third, she had many husbands and was living with a man whom she had not married. Nevertheless, Jesus saw that she had the potential to spread the gospel to her town. Through her, many people came to believe Jesus.

We will explore the gifts and abilities that God has given to us. Many of Jesus' followers were described as sinners, sick people, and outcasts who had been affirmed by Jesus. We will explore ways to affirm one another and to accept affirmation for ourselves.

Bible Memory: 1 Corinthians 12:25

Theological/Biblical Perspective

Women were not highly regarded in the Middle East of Jesus' time. Yet Jesus repeatedly affirmed and encouraged women, as he did other outcasts and people at the bottom of the social ladder.

The history of animosity between Samaria and the southern part of Israel goes way back to the time shortly after Solomon died and Israel split into two kingdoms. Samaritans were considered half-breeds, an impure race that worshiped God in the wrong place. But they were in a double bind. They were not allowed to worship at Jerusalem because they were despised. And they were despised because they did not worship at Jerusalem.

That is why the woman at the well was surprised when Jesus chose to strike up a conversation with her. The intent of the conversation seemed to be to prepare her to bring other Samaritans to see Jesus. When we begin to understand how deep and bitter were the feelings against women and against Samaritans, we begin to understand how radical Jesus' approach was. We can also understand the statement about his disciples when they returned.

Clearly, Jesus saw potential in the woman, potential that prejudice was squelching. Jesus saw her as an instrument of renewal and witness to her people. Though she may not have followed Jesus after this event, she would be called a disciple, just as other women were.

Anticipated Outcomes

- To understand that prejudice can limit a person and affect self-esteem.
- To see God's gifts in other people.
- To find ways to encourage one another to be the persons God intended us to be.

Resources Needed

Grades K–2:
- Very large sheets of paper, enough for two children to lie down on (See people letter exercise in "Responses to the Bible Story.")
- Marker for tracing people letters
- Crayons or paints for coloring

Grades 3–5:
- Hand tools or cutouts of hand tools as described in the puppet play
- Copies of the script

- Paper
- Crayons

Grades 6–8:

- Poster board to make boxes
- Transparent tape to hold box together
- Magazines suitable for cutting out pictures
- Glue
- Cotton swabs, steel wool, toothpicks (to help students add extra symbolic attachments to their collage)

All Grades:

- Pencils and 3″ x 5″ cards

Teacher Preparation

1. Prepare the Bible reading. It is a two-reader piece. Take some time to read it aloud with another person. It might take fifteen to thirty minutes of preparation. A well-executed reading will help the students remember the story. It can be done with a colleague or a student, or two older students can do it.

2. Collect the tools needed for the puppet play for children in the middle grades. If all the tools are not available, cardboard cutouts may be used. Faces and other adornments such as hair should not appear on the tools. The play is designed to present characters that are not a particular gender.

3. Prepare a space for the body lettering for the primary children. If the children will color in the forms with paint, make sure you have old shirts or smocks to cover their regular clothing. Use a plastic ground sheet under the paper they are painting on. In fact, you may want to cover the entire floor with plastic. Instruct the children to work from the top left of their letters toward the bottom right. Doing that will reduce chances of getting paint on clothes. Arrange to have at least one person for every three students painting.

GETTING STARTED

Greet the students as they come in.

Invite everyone to sing stanzas 1 and 2 of "Won't You Let Me Be Your Servant?" (#539 in *The New Century Hymnal* (Cleveland: The Pilgrim Press, 1995). Ask what the song says about how we should act toward other people. List the words and phrases, and ask for the opposite actions from what the song suggests. Which actions do people usually take: the ones suggested in the song, or the opposite ones?

DEVELOPING THE LESSON

Bible Story

READER 1: Today we want to talk about a favorite story of mine.

READER 2: Oh, you mean the one about when you were quacking like a duck . . .

READER 1: *No!*

READER 2: . . . in that restaurant . . .

READER 1: They don't want to hear.

READER 2: . . . with your socks on your ears.

READER 1: Will you stop it! The story I am talking about is the one in the Bible about the woman at the well.

READER 2: Did she wear her socks on her ears?

READER 1: No, but people treated her as though she did.

READER 2: Really? Why?

READER 1: Help me tell the story and you'll find out. Jesus is going back to Galilee and has to travel through Samaria.

READER 2: He and the disciples stop at Sychar, you know, near Jacob's well. So the disciples go into town to shop for groceries and leave Jesus by the well.

READER 1: So this woman comes up to the well to get some water, and Jesus asks her for a drink.

READER 2: She says, "Excuse me? Are you, a man, talking to me, a woman? Are you, a Jew, talking to me, a Samaritan?"

READER 1: In those days being a woman was bad enough, but being a Samaritan woman was considered pretty low on the scale. Men hardly talked to woman they knew, and they never talked to women they didn't know.

READER 2: Jesus says, "Yes, I was talking to you. And if you knew who was talking, you'd have asked me for living water."

READER 1: "You've been in the sun too long! First you start talking to a strange Samaritan woman, and then you want to give me water and you don't have anything to collect it in! Listen, this well is deeper than your average puddle, and our great ancestor Jacob dug it and passed it down to us. Do you think you're better than Jacob is?"

READER 2: "The water you get from here will only do you for a while. The water I give is a real thirst quencher, even to eternal life."

READER 1: "So, if you have this mysterious water, give it to me."

READER 2: "Go and get your husband, and I will."

READER 1: "Well, I don't have a husband."

READER 2: "You got that right. Not only have you been married five times, but you're living with a man who isn't your husband."

READER 1: "Whoa, you're good! But we worship on this mountain, and you Jews insist that Jerusalem is the only place to do that."

READER 2: "That's right. But soon there will be a time when we will all worship God neither here nor there. In fact, that time has already begun. Because God wants us to worship in our hearts."

READER 1: "Well, I'll wait for the Messiah, thanks. Whenever he comes, I'm sure he'll explain all this to me."

READER 2: "I who speak to you am he."

READER 1: She was pretty much impressed with all that and excitedly ran back to her town.

READER 2: She told everyone she had found a man she thought was the Messiah.

READER 1: Many people came to the well, heard Jesus' teachings, and believed.

READER 2: Wow! That's pretty impressive.

READER 1: Yes. Jesus helped the woman to understand, and she was responsible for many others becoming followers.

READER 2: Guess that just goes to show you.

READER 1: You mean that anyone, woman or man, girl or boy, can spread the good news about Jesus Christ, that Jesus looks beyond what other people might see in us and helps us to use our gifts?

READER 2: Yes.

READER 1: Jesus thinks we are important, no matter if we are women, men, girls, or boys?

READER 2: Yes, but also one other thing.

READER 1: What's that?

READER 2: Jesus knew the woman's secrets so that means Jesus knows all about the other story with you and your socks on your ears.

Biblical Reflection

Ask the participants these questions. Encourage as many to share as want to. Remember to acknowledge both genders for their contributions as honestly as you can.

+ What do you think it would have been like for the woman to talk with a strange man who talked the way Jesus talked to her?

+ What was the water that Jesus was talking about?

+ Do you think the woman was liked in her village before she met Jesus?

+ What do you think the people thought of her after they had come to see this man she had been talking to?

+ How do you think the woman felt about the change?

Response Activities

Grades K–2: People Letters

Get out big sheets of newsprint. Tell the children they are to make people letters that spell out a word. People letters are made by two or more children using their bodies to form the letter shapes. The fun will be deciding how the children can work together to make the letter shapes on the newsprint. First, they practice on the floor. For instance, to make the letter "H," two children could lie down beside each other and hold hands. Their bodies could be the vertical parts of the letter, and their touching hands could be the crosspiece. When they have decided how to make a letter, instruct them to lie down on the newsprint, one letter at a time. Trace the letter, and then ask the next group to do their letter. A child may be part of more than one letter if there are more letters in the word than there are children. Choose a word or words that are short but connect to the lesson. You may choose one or more words from the following list or use your own:

Love

God

Friend

Good

Help

Jesus

Or you may want to select short sentences:

♦ God is love.

♦ Jesus is good.

♦ God loves me.

If there is time, allow the children to color the people letter shapes. Affirm them for working together. Tell them that God wants us to work together.

Another Version of People Letters

If large newsprint is not available, but an instantly developing camera is, take pictures of the people letters as the children form them on the floor.

Allow them to draw pictures representing the words or pictures they formed.

Instruct each team to form the letter with their bodies on the floor. Then have them draw the part of the letter that they formed with their bodies. They may make their part as fancy or as colorful as they wish. When they are finished, each child should find the person he or she worked with in forming the body letter. They can then try to put the parts of their drawings together to make a crazy letter. Put the other crazy letters together to make the funniest-looking word they have probably ever seen.

Alternative Activity

Grades 3–5: Puppet Play

The following play uses ordinary hand tools for puppets. If these are not available, cardboard replicas can be made. This show may include other puppets if there are more children. Or it may be done in several teams that could rehearse it and perform it for each other. If the class is small, some of the puppet roles may be combined. You may need to make copies of this script for participants to share.

HAMMER: [*Comes on stage and looks around.*] Wow, I'll never be able to fix up this room in time.

PAINTBRUSH: [*Comes in looking around.*] Wow, I'll never be able to fix up this room in time.

SCREWDRIVER AND RULER: [*Come on simultaneously from opposite sides of the stage and speak at the same time to themselves.*] Wow, I'll never be able to fix up this room in time.

SAW: [*Comes up center stage and looks.*] Wow, I'll never be able to fix up this room in time.

HAMMER: [*Noticing the others.*] What are you all doing here?

RULER: I was asked to fix up this room.

SAW: You! How can a mere ruler fix up a room? I was the one asked to fix up this room.

SCREWDRIVER: Give me a break. All you can do is saw things apart. Besides, everyone knows saws have no brains.

HAMMER: Just like everyone knows how slow screwdrivers are.

RULER: And how bossy hammers are.

SAW: And how narrow rulers are.

PAINTBRUSH: Wait a minute here. Were we all asked to fix this room up?

ALL OTHER TOOLS: I was asked to do it.

PAINTBRUSH: Is anyone here capable of fixing up this room on his or her own?

ALL OTHER TOOLS: I was asked to do it.

PAINTBRUSH: Is anyone here capable of fixing up this room on his or her own? [*Silence.*] I thought so.

HAMMER: So now what? How am I supposed to get this room fixed up when a hammer can't be expected to do everything ?

SAW: Even a saw can't do absolutely everything.

SCREWDRIVER: What will I do?

RULER: I might as well give up and go home.

[*All tools except paintbrush begin to leave.*]

PAINTBRUSH: Wait a minute! Each one of us can do very special things, right?

SAW: [*Looking at the others.*] Yes, I guess that's right.

PAINTBRUSH: Why don't we all work together?

HAMMER: You expect me to work with these tools?

RULER: Hey, that might work. If my friend pencil and I mark the boards to be cut, then saw could cut them and hammer could put them up . . .

HAMMER: . . . with my friends the nails.

SCREWDRIVER: And I can do all kinds of odd jobs. I can do some of the electrical work with my friend pliers. I can even open paint cans for you, brush.

HAMMER: This just might work out okay.

PAINTBRUSH: It feels good to begin to get to know each other. No one is anything like I expected you to be.

HAMMER: Yes, I always thought paintbrushes were weak and frail and not very strong. No one told me you were a good thinker with good ideas.

RULER: I thought all hammers were hardheaded, but I see that's not true.

SCREWDRIVER: I always thought rulers were pretty useless, but not anymore.

SAW: Yes, we all learned the importance of getting to know each other. It makes it easier to work together, and we all made new friends. Say, do you want to go and see hacksaw cut through metal?

Ruler: Through metal? No way!

[*All exit.*]

Ask the class,

* Why couldn't any one of the tools do the job on its own?

* Are any of the tools better than the others?

* How did the tools handle a difficult situation?

* What did you learn from the story?

Here is an alternate response to the lesson: Talk about how the tools learned that working together could get the job done. Ask the class,

* What would have happened if one of the hand tools had tried to do the room all by itself?

* How would one of the tools feel if the others told it that it wasn't wanted, it couldn't do anything right, and nobody wanted to work with it?

• Is that sometimes how we feel or sometimes how we make other people feel?

Encourage the children to draw a picture of one of the tools in the skit cooperating with one of the other tools.

What encouraging things would each tool be saying to the other in the picture?

Think of how another person would feel if he or she was alone. What could the students do to help another person who feels alone because nobody thinks he or she is good enough?

Grades 6–8: Make a Box

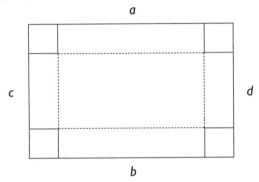

Teacher's instructions: Give each child two 8 ½" x 11" sheets of poster board. Fold the long sides (*a* and *b*) toward each other until the edges touch at the center. Then unfold *a* and *b* and fold *c* and *d* together until the edges touch. Flatten out the poster board, and you should have the pattern shown in the illustration. Cut out the four corners, fold up the sides, and tape them together. Repeat with the second sheet of poster board to make a lid for the box.

From sheets of poster board, cut out the design provided and make a box. After the box is taped together, explain that it is like a collage. The outside of the box represents what the person is like with other people. It is the public self, the side that everyone sees. It also represents the way that a person thinks other people see her or him, which may be different from the way the person wants to be seen. Ask them to use the magazines and cut out pictures that represent the public self and paste them on the outside of the box.

Explain that the inside of the box represents what the person is like inside, the private self. Instruct them to cut out pictures, words, and phrases that represent the private self and paste them on the inside of the box.

After class members have completed their boxes, ask each one about different aspects of the public collage. Ask others what positive things they know or have appreciated about this person. Ask if anyone would like to explain aspects of the private self.

Explain that who we are on the outside and who we are on the inside can be very different. Sometimes we are afraid to let people know who we are on the inside because we feel they won't like us. We may feel they will reject us and we will feel ashamed. The woman at the well had some private things she didn't want Jesus to know. But he knew them anyway. Despite that, he loved her and showed her that she could do something very important for Jesus—tell others about him.

When we tell close friends about our inner selves, they still love us. In fact, the more we know about people, the more special they become. God feels that way too. The more we share our inner selves with God, the more we realize how much we are loved and how special we are.

Give each person a peat pellet and a seed. Encourage students to think of one hope of what they will become. Before they decide, have a time of silent prayer so that they can ask God what they will be.

Explain that the seed represents what God intends for them to become. The peat pellet represents God's Word and teaching. What would happen if they watered the peat pellet, inserted the seed, put it into the box, and closed the lid? What would happen if they left the lid open? Can they see parallels to the way we grow into what God would have us become?

CONCLUDING THE LESSON

Summarize and Evaluate

Provide time for the class to talk about what they have discovered, how they feel, and their questions from today's lesson.

Closing

Give each student a 3" x 5" card and a pencil. On a chalkboard or newsprint, write the words "God," "Love," and "Friend." Tell them to write one sentence for each word. For younger students, ask each one to dictate a sentence about what he or she has learned about that word or feeling that he or she has. For older students, encourage each student to write a sentence for each word that describes his or her feelings about the word.

Collect the cards. Ask the class to pray together, and read the sentences in the form of a prayer.

✳ TEACHING TIP ✳

Behavior and our expectations about behavior sometimes limit boys and girls. Are boys given more freedom to act up because they are boys? When a boy talks excessively or interrupts frequently, how do you react? Do you treat the situation differently if a girl does the same?

We may allow boys to misbehave more than girls. It may be true that girls are better behaved, but that may be because of what they have learned. Girls may be more sensitive to the rules and boundaries than boys are. Often we say, in various ways, "Good girls don't do that."

Be fair in your reaction to the way girls and boys behave. Don't use the excuse, "Oh, that's just that way he is." Try to give a consistent message about expected behavior in the class. Spend some time having the class think about rules they can agree to. Record this list, and remind the class that they agreed to follow these rules. Encourage them to help one another. Use this set of guidelines to help you be fair to everyone.

PARENT TAKE-HOME SHEET

Lesson 5: Exploring Our Potential: Look What I Can Do!

In Today's Lesson

We learned about acknowledging each other's gifts.

We learned that all members of a group have important things to contribute.

We learned that no person or persons are more important than others are.

The group, no matter how large, works best when all work together doing what they do best. This means affirming each other in gifts, not limiting each other according to our gender.

Discussion

This week we have been talking about the importance of thinking about the gifts that God has given us. Sometimes other people do not realize the gifts we have. There are times when we do not realize some of our own gifts because we may not have had an opportunity to try out new things or to be challenged. Or we may not have been given the chance to use them.

God has given each of us unique gifts, and God wants us to discover them and use them. When we keep someone from trying out something new because of gender, we send a message that the person is not good enough. It is better to have the person try and fail than never to have the opportunity. Affirming each other is another way to give people confidence in trying something new.

Family Activity

Cut out the tree, and gather everyone around the table. If there are only two or three people, perhaps you could go around the table twice. Each person is to say something negative, demeaning, or insulting while holding the picture. When the person is finished, she or he is to tear a piece from the picture, keep the piece, and pass the rest of the picture to the next person. The picture goes around the table at least once.

After everyone has had a chance, the remainder of the picture is passed around in reverse order. This time people are asked to say something positive and tape the piece they tore off back to its original place. At the end of the exercise, you will have a very poor replica of the picture you began with because no one will be able to piece the picture together exactly the way it was. It is the same when we hold prejudices and stereotypes about each other. When we believe a stereotype about a person, we are regarding only a small piece of that person. We should try to see the whole person because once we have hurt someone, it is difficult to patch things up.

Parent Tip

Telling jokes about each other that demean our humanness is damaging to all people. You are aware of ethnic jokes that belittle ethnic distinctions as signs of mental, physical, and rational capabilities. These jokes are cruel to other human beings and walk over others' rights by denying them a measure of respect.

The same things can be said for jokes about women. Not only are women treated with little respect in many jokes, they are portrayed as temptresses, stupid, gullible, promiscuous, weak, dependent on men, and docile. Sometimes they are compared to animals in a demeaning way. Jokes about the body often portray women as a collection of body parts to be used at will. Seldom are women portrayed accurately or holistically in jokes. These jokes remind men and women who is considered more valuable and who is less valuable in our society.

If such jokes are told in your child's hearing, take up the challenge to confront the teller. Say that you don't appreciate jokes that demean people, and ask the teller what he (or she) meant by telling that joke. Take some time to explain to your child why you feel this way.

Telling jokes may seem like a small and harmless thing, but over time, when the same message is repeated, it becomes part of what we learn about life. If no one challenges demeaning and "dirty" jokes, our children will grow up believing they are acceptable. More than that, they will continually hear the inner message of these jokes. Women are second-class citizens—or worse.

Set up a fund to challenge the whole family. Ask them to put a dime in a jar every time they hear a joke that demeans women, minorities, and other groups or individuals in society. Agree that you, as parent or guardian, will put in fifty cents for every time the family member confronted the joke teller. Add one dollar if another member of the family was present when the teller was confronted.

What would be a creative way to use this money to stop abuse?

Next Lesson

For men and women to work together, everyone must learn to cooperate with people who are different. The next lesson will be about cooperation, and we will play cooperative games.

Let's Cooperate!

Biblical Text: Luke 10:1–20 (the appointing of the seventy)

Focus: In the last lesson, we began to learn what it takes to work cooperatively. Because it is such an important concept, we want to emphasize that again in this lesson. We hope to recognize that working cooperatively is not always an ideal solution. We are all human, so some mistakes will occur. A person may not do his or her part as well as he or she could. But cooperative work and play teach us to use our imaginative creative skills. We want to teach children to affirm one another, even when things don't go as planned.

Another aspect of cooperative play and work is sharing the credit and the blame. We hope to stress today that the process of working together is more important than the success or failure of the venture. We then want the children to reflect on whether this is true always.

Bible Memory: Luke 10:2

Theological/Biblical Perspective

Here is a passage with a clear lesson. Jesus gave instructions to the seventy about what they were to do. Jesus asked people to work together for the good of the gospel. It is very likely that women were included in this crowd because of Jesus' attitude to women and their potential for ministry. Would women go out together? Would Jesus send out a man-and-woman team? These are some things to think about during the lesson. Jesus made it plain that the work was urgent because "the harvest is plentiful."

In what way can men and women work together today using this sending as an example? Jesus prepared them for failure. If they were not accepted, it was not their fault. Neither one of the team needed to shoulder the blame. In fact, Jesus set things up so that no one had to waste time placing or accepting blame. The result seemed to be that more energy could be directed to the important work at hand. Blaming can be seen as evil's way of disrupting a good work. Jesus' vision of Satan falling might in part have been due to the fact that people were not sidetracked from their assignment. Laboring together for a single purpose worked—and all to the praise and glory of God.

Anticipated Outcomes

- To learn that working together pleases God.
- To create good things and be effective by working cooperatively.
- To learn that cooperation is more important than success or failure.
- To teach and learn from each other.

✳ TEACHING TIP ✳

It is always a struggle to give children a fair chance to share their insights and responses. Sometimes there are children who are more aggressive in their sharing, while some may be more withdrawn. Some children need to talk almost immediately, and others need time to process and think.

Many times (certainly not always) these behaviors follow gender lines. Boys tend to be more aggressive in their verbal skills, and girls seem to need time for processing information. Because class time is limited, we feel the need to move on and not give everyone a chance to interact with questions or responses to the story. Perhaps a simple rule such as allowing one person to share only twice during the lesson may help in hearing from everyone. Perhaps there can be time in between the story and the reflection for the children to think and process what they have heard. Then if a verbal response is required, make a special effort to ask specific girls to answer first. Affirm each child every time he or she contributes.

Resources Needed

Read the exercises in the "Response Activity" section to compile a list of the items needed.

General:

- Signs with identification numbers for each station
- Cardboard backing for each station
- A sheet of paper and a pencil for each team

Station 1:

- Hammer, board
- Different-size nails (larger nails for younger children)

Station 2:

- Markers
- Construction paper

Station 3:

- Jar filled with beans, pennies, or similar object (count before session)

Station 4: No special materials needed.

Station 5:

- Large doll
- Two diapers and safety pins

Station 6:

- Building blocks

Station 7:

- Ball (larger size for younger children)

Station 8: No special materials needed.

Teacher Preparation

1. Set up activity stations: #1: Hammer a Nail; #2: Say It Backward; #3: Guess the Beans; #4: How Many?; #5: Change the Baby; #6: Tower; #7: Nose Ball; and #8: Household Appliance.

2. Gather the necessary equipment (see lists above), and put it at each center area.

3. Write out the instructions for each activity. Then cut them out, paste them on sheets of cardboard, and post them at the appropriate area.

4. Set up the stations around the walls of a large room or on an outside space. The best arrangement will depend on the space available. Perhaps having them in a circle will be least confusing. Then each team could begin at a different station and move clockwise until it has visited all the stations.

GETTING STARTED

Greet everyone. Divide into intergenerational groups. Then direct the groups to sit together to listen to the Bible story.

DEVELOPING THE LESSON

Explain that many passages in the Bible describe men and women cooperating to bring the good news to people. One of these passages is Luke 8:1–15.

Bible Story: The "Faith in Action" Talk Show Skit

Ask for volunteers to read parts in this skit.

FAITH: Welcome to the "Faith in Action" talk show. My name is Faith. Today we are interviewing some of Jesus' followers. We have Bartholomew, one of the twelve disciples, Joanna, and Susanna. Welcome. Could each of you tell us what you do?

SUSANNA: I pick up odd jobs here and there. I do some sheep shearing, some sewing, some cloth making.

BART: I just hang around with Jesus. Mostly I try to figure out what he's trying to teach us. That's a full-time job, let me tell you.

JOANNA: I follow Jesus whenever I can. My husband is the manager of Herod's household, so I get lots of time to myself.

FAITH: Well, how do you all survive? It seems as if Susanna here is the only one with even a part-time job.

BART: Oh, there are more of us. If it weren't for women like these two, we wouldn't be able to do half the things we do.

JOANNA: Being in the king's house, my husband is very well paid. I simply use part of our savings to help buy food and sometimes pay for shelter, depending on where we travel.

FAITH: So what is one of the most interesting parts of being with Jesus?

SUSANNA: He appreciates you for who you are and what your gifts are. Many of the women had some sort of disease or disability or problem that Jesus cured, so of course we appreciate the miracle healings because each of us experienced one.

JOANNA: Yes, but I like his stories too. Especially the one about the sower and the soil. It's the one where the sower spreads grain. The seed that fell on the path didn't grow because the ground was too hard and it got trampled and the birds ate the grain. Some seed was thrown among the rocks, where there wasn't enough moisture . . .

SUSANNA: . . . and some was thrown among the thorns, which choked whatever grew there. But some fell on good soil and gave a good crop.

FAITH: But what does it mean?

BART: The seed is the Word of God. We have to watch that the devil doesn't take the Word from us like the seed on the path. The seed in the rocks warns us to be nurtured and let the Word take root. The seed in the thorns means that worldly things can choke out the meaning of the Word. The grain that grew is the Word of God growing in our hearts and spreading to others.

FAITH: So Jesus wants everyone to spread the gospel, the Word of God?

JOANNA: That's right. Whether people are rich or poor, men, women, boys, girls, no matter what race, or how old, healthy, or sick—anyone can obey the Word of God.

SUSANNA: Anyone can be one of Christ's disciples.

BART: Right.

FAITH: Well, thank you for that insightful look at life with Jesus. It seems that Jesus did not assign tasks according to what others thought men could do or women could do. It seems Jesus looked for the unique gifts of his followers and thought they would do their best work by cooperating with one another. What do you think about that, girls and boys?

What do you think Jesus would have had women and men do?

Songs: "Women Disciples" and "Men Disciples"

Introduce the songs by explaining that both men and women were disciples of Jesus. Look over the lists of disciples in the songs.

Response Activity: Cooperative Games

Here are some suggestions for cooperative games. You may think of more. Adapt these activities to suit your situation.

Set up a series of centers with instructions at each center describing the task to be performed. The teams go from one center to the next until everyone has been to each center. Give them a master list with the number of centers listed, and ask one person in each team to mark down the scores. Each center's activities are designed to allow each member of the team a chance to participate. Teams of two to five persons do this set of tasks. You may have to make sure that each team does the tasks an equal number of times, which means teams with fewer members will do it more times. Divide the groups so that there is a mix of ages and genders.

#1: Hammer a Nail

Each team member must hammer a nail completely flat into a board. Encouragement is the only help, except for possibly getting the nail started. Different-size nails may be used for different age groups. Mark 1 point for every hammer blow.

#2: Say It Backward

Make a list of each person's name on the team printed backward. The team must learn to pronounce the backward names so that they can say them in unison out loud. Score 1 point if you can do it without laughing, 10 points if you can't. Add 20 points if you are not successful at getting everyone to say the names backward.

#3: Guess the Beans

Fill a large jar with beans, pennies, or similar items. Ask each team member to guess how many objects are in the jar. Each person should guess without consulting the other members and write the estimate on a piece of paper. One person adds up the total and takes the average as the official team guess. At the end of the contest, give the actual number. The team that comes the closest to the actual number will be able to deduct 25 points from any of the other stations.

#4: How Many?

Tell each team to go to the sanctuary or worship area and estimate how many people could be seated if the place was as full as possible. The team closest to the actual number will be allowed to deduct 15 points from any other station.

#5: Change the Baby

This will require two people, one to hold the diaper and one to change the doll. Each team of two must take one diaper off and put another on, so there should be two diapers. Mark down each person's time. Then add up the total time for your team. Convert that into total seconds.

#6: Tower

Using building blocks, each team must build a tower by putting one block on top of another. Each team member places a block until the tower falls.

The team must count the number of blocks left over as the tower is built. If you use all the blocks, take 20 points off any other exercise.

#7: Nose Ball

In relay style, team members are to push a ball with their noses a required distance and then back again. One person may time the teams. Note the total time and convert it to seconds.

#8: Household Appliance

The team decides to act out the function of a household appliance. Keep it simple, for example, the furnace, the stove, or the iron. Include everyone in the process. Perform as these appliances for the other teams when the other events have been completed. If no one can guess your appliance, give your team 25 points. If others guess correctly, score 0 points.

Final Scoring

See what the final scores for teams are. The teams with the lowest scores are the ones that collaborated and cooperated the best. Congratulations!

CONCLUDING THE LESSON

Summarize and Evaluate

Ask members from each age group to share some things they learned in this lesson.

Bring the class together with the new songs learned today.

Closing

Encourage everyone to stand in a circle and repeat the following litany:

[*Point to self.*] I am a special creation of God.
[*Point to person on the right.*] You are a special creation of God.
[*Point to all the others in the circle.*] We are all special in God's sight.
I want to treat others fairly.
I want to affirm each person's gifts.
God's gifts are given to boys and girls.
There are no bad gifts or good gifts.
Each person was given gifts to help others.
God meant for us to work together.

PARENT TAKE-HOME SHEET

Lesson 6: Let's Cooperate!

In Today's Lesson

Today we learned more about how to work cooperatively. Cooperation is difficult to do consistently, although we all usually agree it is a good thing to do. Perhaps we feel it will take too much time or the end result will not be exactly as we had hoped or planned. Cooperation would mean listening to others and perhaps incorporating what they say and the suggestions they make.

We may need to learn new things. We as grown-ups often are uncomfortable learning new things, especially if children are the ones teaching us. But learning and working together cooperatively can be fun as well as great family get-together time.

Discussion Questions

- What are the advantages of working cooperatively?
- What things can you learn?
- What are the challenges of working cooperatively?

Family Activity

Use these suggestions of projects to do together, and add ideas of your own. Choose one project that everyone can participate in, and find out who would like to do what. The card-making project is broken down into skills for you to suggest how people can contribute in a cooperative way. The other projects are left for you to fill in cooperative skills that may be needed. Schedule time for this project in the coming week. Plan the first learning time as soon as possible.

1. Making Cards

Everyone likes to receive a card for a birthday or another special occasion or during an illness. Take an opportunity to make some generic cards that can be used in any situation so that they will be available when needed. People appreciate homemade cards because of the time and thought put into making them.

Cooperative skills needed:

- Someone to cut out pictures from old magazines.
- Someone to draw pictures and color them.

- Someone to design cards. (All of them don't have to be rectangular or square. Some cards could have cutout windows.)

- Someone to think of words to put on the card, both the outside and the inside.

- Someone to design and make envelopes. (Take apart an envelope to see how it's done, check in books on origami paper folding, or invent your own style.)

2. Spring Cleaning

A room or rooms in the house need cleaning. This could include new ways to organize a room.

Room or rooms:

Cooperative skills needed:

3. Special Letter

Create a letter on audiotape or videotape to someone who lives at a distance. This could include jokes, stories, or musical numbers, based on people's talents.

Cooperative skills needed:

4. Baking for a Special Person or Occasion

Cooperative skills needed:

5. Planning a Miniholiday, Family Outing, or Picnic

Cooperative skills needed:

6. Taking Part in a Ministry of the Church

The ministry could be janitorial work, day care, or a senior citizens' program.

Cooperative skills needed:

There are other ways that family members can participate in projects. What ways can you think of?

Information for Parents

Cooperative work can be slow at first, especially if children are learning new skills. Factor in the time difference when doing things cooperatively. Attempt small projects at first with a high probability of ease and success. Celebrate the completed task in a simple but affirming way, such as a group hug or time playing outdoors or at table games together.

The time, effort, and patience you display at the beginning help the children know they are important. If there are decisions to be made, look for ways to include everyone in the process. Even though you may have to make the final decision, perhaps each person could give his or her opinion.

Be supportive during the task. Treat failures, setbacks, and mistakes as times for learning. Humor will smooth things over. Be forgiving, assume everyone is trying his or her best, and affirm wherever you can. In a world of growing individuality, learning to work cooperatively is an important skill.

Next Lesson

We will discuss how gender affects the way we relate to one another.

APPENDIX

Women Disciples

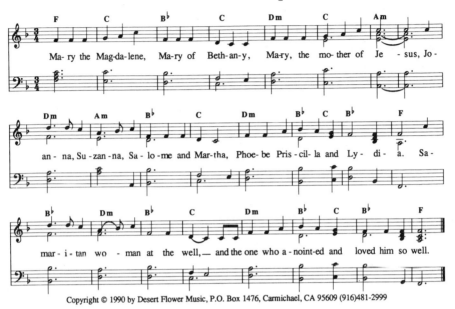

Ma- ry the Mag-da-lene, Ma-ry of Beth-an-y, Ma-ry, the mo-ther of Je - sus, Jo-
an- na, Su-zan-na, Sa- lo-me and Mar-tha, Phoe-be Pris-cil- la and Ly- di- a. Sa-
mar-i-tan wo - man at the well,— and the one who a-noint-ed and loved him so well.

Copyright © 1990 by Desert Flower Music, P.O. Box 1476, Carmichael, CA 95609 (916)481-2999

Men Disciples

words and music
by Jim Strathdee

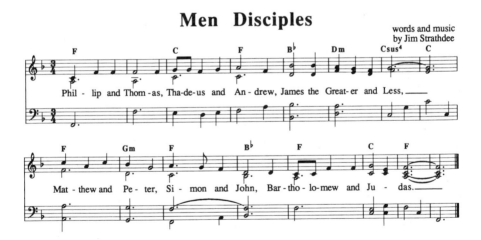

Phil - lip and Thom -as, Tha-de-us and An - drew, James the Great-er and Less,___
Mat - thew and Pe- ter, Si - mon and John, Bar-tho- lo-mew and Ju - das.___

"Women Disciples," words and music by Jean and Jim Strathdee. Copyright © 1990 by Desert Flower Music, P.O. Box 1476, Carmichael CA 95609. "Men Disciples," words and music by Jim Strathdee. Copyright © 1990 by Desert Flower Music, P.O. Box 1476, Carmichael CA 95609. Both used by permission.

Understanding One Another

Biblical Text: Mark 12:28–34

Focus: Through this lesson, we learn better how people can relate to one another. We also learn about how gender influences ways that people relate to one another.

Bible Memory: Mark 12:29–31

Theological/Biblical Perspective

Unlike the other encounters between Jesus and the scribes, the incident recorded in Mark 12:28–34 begins with a request to Jesus to settle a dispute about the law. The scribes and rabbis organized the six hundred laws according to fundamental principles. A scribe asks Jesus what he believes is the most important commandment.

Jesus begins by quoting Deuteronomy 6:4–5, which forms the opening of the Jewish daily prayer, the Shema. Jesus affirms that the most important commandment is to love God. Second, Jesus quotes from Leviticus 19:18. He reminds us that we are called to love others as we love ourselves.

Loving others was not a new concept to Jewish scholars of that time. The Hebrew Scriptures are filled with admonishments and commandments to love the neighbor and forgive the enemy. Jesus agrees with the scribe and makes it clear that Christian love is rooted in the traditional laws of the Hebrew faith.

Jesus reminds us that the commandment to love our neighbors is second only to the commandment to love God. Loving others means that we are called by our faith to treat others with respect and care. Discriminating against others because of their gender cannot be part of God's plan for loving others.

The purpose of this lesson is to remember that we are called by God's love to care for those who are different. Sometimes our stereotypes of girls and boys stand in the way of caring for one another and treating each person as an individual. This lesson will help the students practice skills overcoming stereotypes and increase their understanding of how gender influences relationships.

Anticipated Outcomes

- To learn that our response to God's love is to love others just as we are called to love ourselves.
- To increase students' understanding of how gender roles influence how people relate to one another.
- To learn ways to communicate better between genders.

Resources Needed

Grades K–2, Grades 3–5, and Grades 6–8:

- Poster board
- Markers and tape
- Two sheets and pins
- Paper and pencils

Grades 3–5:

- Copies of the "Dear Gertrude" letters

Grades 6–8 and Optional Activity:

- Paper and pencils
- Packages and suitcases marked "Hate," "Prejudice," and "Anger" for the opening sketch

Teacher Preparation

(Grades 6–8) 1. Ask two adults—a male and a female—to volunteer for an experiment in this class. Be familiar with the activity so that you can describe it to them.

(Grades 6–8) 2. Cut a poster board into 3-inch-wide strips. Write the following words and phrases onto appropriate lengths: "kind to pets," "loves children," "strong muscles," "anxious," "frightened of insects," "great driver," "likes fishing," "plays sports," "likes hiking," "loves to sing," "plays a musical instrument." The teacher will want to ask the guests some characteristics such as hobbies, which will make the phrases more specific. Save some blank cardboard pieces for suggestions by the class.

(Grades 3–5) 3. Copy "Dear Gertrude" letters.

4. Recruit two adults to act out the opening sketch. Prepare the suitcases and packages for Person 1 to carry.

GETTING STARTED

Gather the group together to listen to the opening sketch.

Opening Sketch

Person 1 walks in the door carrying large packages and suitcases. Each package should be labeled with a word such as "hate," "prejudice," "anger," "hurt feelings," "loneliness," or "suspicion."

PERSON 2: Hey! Where are you going?

PERSON 1: No place in particular. I'm just wandering around.

PERSON 2: Just wandering around . . . you look as if you are carrying a heavy load.

PERSON 1: Not really. It doesn't seem that heavy. I've been carrying this load for a long time. I'm used to it.

PERSON 2: You must be strong.

PERSON 1: I guess you are right.

PERSON 2: Would you mind showing me what you are carrying?

PERSON 1: Not at all. I'm kind of proud of everything that I can carry. Let's see here. I've got this package of hate. That was one of my first packages to pick up.

PERSON 2: Where did you find a package like that to carry?

PERSON 1: I can't quite remember when I got this package. I just know that I was really young. Somebody did something to me. It really made me mad, and I decided that I would carry this package wherever I go—just in case I needed it. You know.

PERSON 2: No, I don't know. What would you need it for?

PERSON 1: Well, just in case you meet someone who is different or just in case you meet someone who might do something bad to you, you want to be prepared.

PERSON 2: Prepared for what?

PERSON 1: Prepared for the worst. Ready to fight. Armed to the teeth. No second chances.

PERSON 2: Why not prepare for the best?

PERSON 1: You can't be serious! I mean, look at some of these other packages I have here. Why, I've got a good amount of anger. That will help in a fight. I've also got prejudice. That's just to keep me prepared to meet people who are different.

PERSON 2: It seems to me that you are pretty loaded down.

PERSON 1: I don't feel loaded down. Well, I guess there are times I feel a little burdened. But I know that I'm always prepared.

PERSON 2: You're prepared, all right. You're prepared to fight. But what happens if you meet someone you like? I think your anger, your prejudice, and your hate might get in the way.

PERSON 1: I never thought of it that way. I guess I would like not having to carry these packages all the time. But I don't know how to put them down.

PERSON 2: I think I can help you. Why don't you try putting down one of the packages? I'll tell you what . . . I'll walk with you. While we walk, I'll tell you about Jesus. Jesus had a special message of love and caring. Jesus said that the love of God is reflected in our care for others. I think that knowing more about Jesus will help you put all of those packages down.

PERSON 1: [*Putting a large package down.*] Hey, I do feel as if my burden's been lifted a little. I think I would like to know more about Jesus.

The two people walk out of the room talking. Person 1 can put down another package as he or she leaves the room.

DEVELOPING THE LESSON

Explain that today's lesson is going to be on understanding one another better. Perhaps we, too, can set aside some of our prejudice and anger.

Bible Study: Mark 12:28–34

Tell the class the story of the scribe asking Jesus the question about which commandment is the most important. Discuss these scriptures with the class.

> In Jesus' time there were people called scribes. Today we might call them lawyers. Scribes knew the laws very well. Now one day there was a scribe who came up to Jesus and asked, "Which commandment is the first of all?"
>
> Jesus said, "The most important commandment is to love God with all your heart, soul, mind, and strength. [Which means we are to love God more than anyone or anything.] The second most important commandment is to love your neighbor as much as you love yourself. [Which means we are supposed to really love our neighbors because we love ourselves very much.]"
>
> The scribe was amazed. He said, "Jesus, you hit the nail on the head. The two commandments you named are much more important than burnt offerings and such."
>
> Jesus smiled at the scribe and said, "You're not only smart; you're wise. You aren't far from the realm of heaven." The scribe smiled, too, because Jesus had just given him a mighty big compliment and he felt good.

Reflections

Do the reflections in grade groupings.

Grades K–2:

- What did Jesus mean when he said that we are supposed to love our neighbors?

- Who are our neighbors? Those who live near us? Family? Classmates? Others?

- Do you remember any other stories that Jesus told about loving our neighbors?

- We've been talking about how boys and girls get along. What would Jesus say about how boys and girls get along?

- Can you think of times when you treated someone of the other gender in a way that Jesus would like?

Grades 3–5:

- Review the scripture with the class. (See discussion questions with younger children.)

- What does our society tell us about how boys and girls should treat one another?

- How do the kids you know treat one another?

- Can boys and girls be friends?

- What kinds of pressure do kids feel to treat one another in ways that are not respectful and caring?

Grades 6–8:

- Review the scripture with the class. (See discussion questions with younger children.)

- Can you think of some examples when boys have mistreated girls?

- Can you think of some examples when girls have mistreated boys?

- Why are girls sometimes afraid of boys?

- In what ways do girls sometimes make boys afraid?

- What suggestions do you have for both boys and girls to get along better?

Response Activities

Grades K–2: Overlapping Circles

Draw three overlapping circles on newsprint. On one circle, write "Boys." On the others, write "Girls" and "Adults." Invite each group member to put his or her "Friendly Face" on the part of the circle representing his or her answer. Ask the group members to finish this sentence: "I have friends who are . . ."

Show the students how one circle represents that they have friends who are boys. The overlapping parts represent someone who has friends who are boys and friends who are girls. The very center represents someone who has boys, girls, and adults as friends.

Ask them to place their "Friendly Faces" to complete these and other sentences:

"At church I have friends who are . . ."

"In church school I have friends who are . . ."

"In my neighborhood I have friends who are . . ."

"In my school I have friends who are . . ."

"In my music/dancing/sports activities I have friends who are . . ."

Discuss the various areas where children have friends, and point out how they may have different friends in each area.

Grades 3–5: "Dear Gertrude"

Divide the class into groups. Together read the unsigned letters. Tell each group to pick one letter to which to write a response. Is the writer a girl or a boy? Write a response if the writer is a boy. Write another response if the writer is a girl. Be prepared to explain your answers.

Invite each group to read its responses. Discuss the answers:

- Is the writer really a boy or a girl?
- Why did you think a girl or a boy was the writer?
- How are the responses different?
- Does it make a difference?

Grades 6–8: Change the Gender of the People in the Parable

Divide the class into smaller groups. Assign each group one of the following parables: the talents (Matt. 25:14–30); the loving father (Luke 15:11–32); the shrewd steward (Luke 16:1–15); the lost silver piece (Luke 15:8–10); finding the lost sheep (Luke 15:4–7). Encourage each group to read the parable carefully. Think about how the parable would be different if the men were women and the women were men. Instead of writing out the story, turn it into a short play.

Ask each group to present its version, and discuss the different versions that the class created. Here are some questions for students to consider:

- How might women have handled the conflict differently?
- What ideas could women and men have shared that would have lessened the conflict?
- Is the meaning of the parable changed?
- What details needed to be changed to be consistent with the gender changes?

All Grades: Describe Women and Men

For this activity, ask the male and female guests to sit in two chairs at the front of the classroom. Gently wrap a sheet loosely around each guest so that only his or her head shows. Pin the sheet so that the guests can take their arms out later in the activity.

Explain to the group that without knowing the characteristics of the particular two people, the class will guess who has the following characteristics. Use the poster board phrases/words that have been prepared ahead of time. Tape the phrases onto the sheet.

Use the blank cardboard pieces for class suggestions.

After all the characteristics have been attached to each person, encourage each guest to share about whether these characteristics really match his or her personality. The class will discover that both people share some characteristics.

Discuss which characteristics the class attributed to one person or another because of gender.

Optional Activity

Grades 3–5 and Grades 6–8: Describe Stereotypes of Boys and Girls

Divide a piece of newsprint into three columns. On the left, ask the class to name the characteristics of men in general (possible responses: "strong," "business minded," "warriorlike," "confrontational"). On the right, ask the class to name the characteristics of women in general (possible responses: "caring," "loving," "helpful," "weak," "soft-spoken," "compromising").

Then in the middle column, list the characteristics of Jesus (possible responses: "kind," "loving," "healing," "caring").

Discuss the similarities and differences.

CONCLUDING THE LESSON

Summarize and Evaluate

Gather the class together to spend a few minutes recalling what has happened in this lesson. Answer questions, and give the class some ideas about what will happen in the next lesson.

Closing

Explain that the class will end with prayer. After a few minutes of silence, each person can say one word from the lesson today. Words could be "love," "God," and "Jesus," among others. Close the prayer by saying, "Thank you, God, for loving each of us."

✳ TEACHING TIP ✳

Take some time to look over the materials, toys, and pictures that are used in the church school classroom. Do the materials represent a variety of people from different cultures, races, and countries? Are the dolls representative of the varieties of races in the world? Are people of a variety of ages—children, grown-ups, and older people—depicted in a variety of occupations and roles? Are men and women shown in a variety of roles?

The images that we show children give them information about others and themselves. Children can overcome their fears about differences through contact with others. They can begin this process by seeing images of differences as "normal" or ordinary. This happens when teachers and other are conscious of the images the children see.

Therefore, it is important to look closely at images. Find a good time to sort the church school program pictures. Some pictures may need to be replaced. Add pictures of families in a variety of shapes: grandmother and children, or dad and children. Replace some of the pictures of the classic family: mom, dad, and two children. Add pictures of people from different races. Replace pictures that have all white people. Be sure that disabled people are included in the pictures. Add women doing a variety of jobs. Add men doing helpful tasks in the home. Show children varieties of images.

PARENT TAKE-HOME SHEET

Lesson 7: Understanding One Another

In Today's Lesson

We learned that our response to God's love is to love others just as we are called to love ourselves (Mark 12:28–34).

We increased our understanding of how gender roles influence the ways that people relate to one another.

We learned ways to communicate better between genders.

Discussion Points

* Look at the scripture from this lesson.

* Ask each family member to name a neighbor.

* Share experiences in which boys or girls felt unfairly treated.

Family Activity

A Family Time Capsule

As a family, you will have an opportunity to pack a time capsule. It will hold items that will represent this time and age. You will close this capsule and not open it for five years. After that period of time, the family can open the container and see what was saved.

First, clean and dry a gallon white plastic bleach bottle. Ask each person to put into the bottle small items that represent herself or himself. In keeping with the theme of this lesson, look for items that represent loving relationships and things that help break down gender stereotyping. Some suggestions would be family pictures, personal letters, or other items. In addition, newspaper articles about conflict or unfair treatment of others or efforts at combating gender stereotypes could be added to the time capsule.

As items are gathered, tell family members the significance of each item. Close the container and glue the following label on the front. Put this container somewhere safe. Open in five years. See if the world is a more loving place.

OUR FAMILY'S TIME CAPSULE

On this _____ day of _____ in the year _____, we, the _____ family, put these items in this time capsule. Our wish and prayer are that peace will come to all the earth. That all people will be loved and cared for. That the world will be a better place for boys and girls. We will open this time capsule in five years on _____ [date].

Information for Parents

"Actions speak louder than words." That old saying is certainly true. It is important to say the proper things to our children and to act in proper ways. Think about the actions that subtly tell children that one group is inferior or another group is superior. Do we, as parents, always praise certain kinds of people? Do we signal to our children that certain people make us uncomfortable or fearful?

Teaching our children to love all people means confronting our own prejudices and biases. We have to be honest with ourselves and look at the attitudes that we learned in childhood. We are forced to examine our actions and behavior and look for clues that we aren't always as loving and caring as we would hope to be.

Teaching Christian values to children means being intentional about what we do and say. It also means praying for guidance and following Jesus' example. That often means working hard on improving our behavior and learning new patterns of behavior.

Next Lesson

The next lesson will focus on stereotypes and how the media influence ways that we see others.

APPENDIX

"Dear Gertrude"

1. Dear Gertrude,

I have a problem at school. Just yesterday I was sent to the principal's office for fighting. Every day this boy bothers me. He calls me names and tries to steal my lunch money. I told him to bug off. But he won't stop. Yesterday I lost my temper and slugged him. What should I do now?

Sent to the Principal's Office

2. Dear Gertrude,

Tell me what to do. My sister has been taking things from my room. First I noticed that my T-shirts were disappearing. Then I discovered that she was taking stamps out of my collection. If I tell her I know she's doing it, she will only deny it. How can I handle this situation?

Stamp Collector

3. Dear Gertrude,

Sports are the greatest things in the world. I love basketball and soccer, but most of all I love football. But the neighborhood boys won't let me play. They say that I'm too little. I know that I'm small, but I'm really fast and I think I would really help the team. Tell me what to do.

Left-out Football Player

4. Dear Gertrude,

Aunt Susie is coming to visit next week. She is a very nice woman, but she loves to pat my head and give me sloppy kisses. It is embarrassing. What should I do?

Slobbered On in Iowa

5. Dear Gertrude,

I am a nervous wreck in school. The boys don't seem to like me. They never ask me to be on a team. They don't seem to want to ride bikes with me, and they ignore me. How can I make them feel like I can play too?

Ignored in School

6. Dear Gertrude,

My parents are getting a divorce. I can't seem to talk to anyone about it. All day long that's all I think about. I feel like crying in every class. But I know the kids will laugh at me. Where can I go to get help?

Laughing Instead of Crying

Media and Stereotypes

Biblical Text: Mark 8:34–9:1 or Matthew 16:24–28 (cost of following Jesus)

Focus: This week we want to raise awareness of how the media form our opinions and our self-worth. The media strongly influence our lives. We are not attempting to dump blame on the media. But a proper understanding of the media and the effects on us will equip children to discern lies and distortions in other areas of their lives. Today we will help children discover the lies that they see and hear about gender stereotypes. Especially relevant are the images of what is feminine and what is masculine. What do television, radio, and print materials tell us about men and women?

Bible Memory: Matthew 16:24a, d

Theological/Biblical Perspective

In this passage we see Jesus warning his followers about some of the pitfalls awaiting them as they attempt to follow him. In the world there are endless side roads to take and paths to lead one astray. This passage conveys the idea that followers must be firm, intentional, and consistent in their choices. Those who choose Christ will need to give up old ways and habits. These followers will have to be vigilant because the world never gives up. There is a need to realize that something larger than life here on earth is at stake, and that is the soul.

Anticipated Outcomes

- To identify the lies that we encounter in the media about gender.
- To become more aware of how we are affected by gender stereotyping in the media.
- To learn to think critically about what we see and hear.

Resources Needed

Grades K–2:

- Two or three children's storybooks, preferably about people rather than animals
- Crayons and paper for drawing and coloring

Grades 3–5:

- TV and VCR
- Tape of popular TV show including commercials
- Copies of the "Television Activity Page" (page 92)
- Plain paper and colored pencils or markers

Grades 6–8:

- Old magazines with lots of ads (*Life, Maclean's, Time, Good Housekeeping*)
- Paper and pencils

Teacher Preparation

Paste some ads on the door to the classroom, or mount a poster of a collage of ads on the door. Play loud music or turn up a radio. Turn on the TV, and open newspapers and magazines on the tables to the advertisements.

1. Students in primary grades: Practice reading the stories.

2. Students in middle grades: Photocopy the "Television Activity Page." You will need one copy for each group of three or four people.

3. Junior youth: Select several stereotypical ads as examples for the class.

GETTING STARTED

Have a TV or radio on with the volume turned up. Welcome the class, and move the girls to one side and the boys to the other.

In spite of the noise, introduce the lesson, and ask for silent prayer. Bow your head for a moment, and then get everyone's attention. Tell the students you can't concentrate, and then ask them to turn off whatever is on and close all the magazines. Sit for a few moments in silence. Then pray, "Thank you, God, that we can get away from the noise and the signs of advertising and be quiet with you. Help us to look at our lives to see what is important. Help us to discover the lies in advertising. Amen."

Explain that advertising can reach us wherever we are. Advertising tries to tell us the things we need to make us happy. But the things that are advertised won't make us happy. We will only want more. Following Jesus is a difficult choice, but it helps us set priorities in life that are more important than the priorities advertisers want us to set.

DEVELOPING THE LESSON

Readers' Theater

READER 1: Well, I'm off!

READER 2: Where are you going?

READER 1: To follow Jesus. Wanna come?

READER 2: Nah, I got a ball game tonight. How long will you be gone?

READER 1: The rest of my life likely. At least that's what I'm counting on.

READER 2: All your . . . isn't this kinda sudden?

READER 1: Oh, I've given it plenty of thought, and Jesus himself wants me to go along. I want to get to know people and get to know myself and find out how I can do what Jesus wants.

READER 2: But you can have that right here! You don't have to go trotting around the country with that . . . carpenter. Besides, you can't go off like this. It's not what any respectable woman (or man) would do.

READER 1: Should I be acting more like the advertisements on TV, in the paper, on the radio, in magazines?

READER 2: At least that would be more normal.

READER 1: That's where you are wrong. All of the things about men and women that we see in commercials and on TV shows are lies. They not only lie about what will make me happy; they lie about what people are really like.

READER 2: What are you talking about?

READER 1: They try to tell me girls are not as smart as boys; boys are stronger than girls; boys don't cry; girls always cry; boys don't have to dress up; girls have to look pretty and be thin; boys worry about playing games, buying cars, and being cool; girls worry about attracting boys; women do all the work at home; boys are bratty; girls are well behaved; boys seem to always come up with the better ideas; men always save women from danger and take risks and display bravery; and women are being rescued and helped by men. Those things are what I call stereotypes.

READER 2: But they are harmless, aren't they?

READER 1: When people see and hear these things often enough, they believe they're true. Men and women, boys and girls, get the wrong ideas about how God wants them to act. Jesus is saying that we have to get away from all that in order to find out how to live with one another according to God's will.

READER 2: But if that really is all a lie, then what are we supposed to do?

READER 1: Look, if we want to live together in a more peaceful way, we have to get to know one another. I know that men and women are not the same, but I also know that each of us has important gifts. I just want to get to know the person, not believe what someone else tells me. That is my choice. Jesus will accept you, even if you can't give up all you possess. But you have to know that following Jesus is not easy and it won't always be fun. People will think you are nuts, crazy, off your rocker. But you will have God as a personal Friend, and you'll get to know some other wonderful people who think that God's friendship is worth giving up a few things for.

READER 2: Can I think about this?

READER 1: Better you should talk with Jesus. The more you think about it, the less likely you are to act. If you hear God calling, the time to act is *now*.

READER 2: Where is this Jesus?

READER 1: Follow me!

READER 2: I must be crazy to even be thinking about this.

READER 1: Welcome to the club.

For reflection:

- Are Jesus' ways that different from what we actually do? How?
- Are Jesus' ways that much different from what we see in advertisements? How?

Response Activities

Grades K–2: Pick any two children's storybooks to read aloud to the students. Ask them to think about what would happen in a specific part of the story if the gender of the character was changed. Encourage them to draw a picture that would illustrate the new situation.

Ask, "I wonder what would have happened if the character of Jeffrey was a girl named Cindy (or if Melissa was a boy named Raymond)?"

Grades 3–5: Using the VCR, show a fifteen-minute clip of a popular TV program. Include the ads that appear. Direct the students to fill out the "Television Activity Page" and share their findings. Invite them to compare what girls in the group saw and what boys in the group saw. Was there a difference? If there was, encourage them to reflect on why.

Grades 6–8: Cut out ads that objectify women and men. Hygiene care products, liquor and beer ads, cigarette ads, car ads, and others use women and sometimes men to sell the products. Sometimes the ad will show only one part of the body or portray a person in a seductive pose or in scanty clothing. Sometimes a man and a woman will be shown in an "intimate" moment. Many times these images have little or nothing to do with the product.

Ask each person to choose an ad and write down what the ad says about men or women and the relationship between men and women. Who is dressed nicer or "sexier"? If a man and a woman are in the picture, who is higher and who is lower in the picture? What does the ad tell us about standards for beauty? What does it say about a man's role? A woman's role? Are these role suggestions true in real life? Are they fair to men and women? Do the class members see the lies portrayed in ads as discrimination?

What's in a Song?

Ask the students to name a favorite song.

- Does it feature a male singer, a female singer, or both?
- What is the song about?
- What does the song tell you about females?
- What does the song tell you about males?

What is a favorite TV ad?

- Is the person doing the selling a male or female?

- Are there other males or females in the ad? What are they doing?

- What does the ad tell you about the product?

- What does the ad tell you about females?

- What does the ad tell you about males?

Discuss some of your findings.

Optional Activity

Grades 3–5: Write a Television Commercial

Ask a team of boys and girls to write and act out a television commercial.

CONCLUDING THE LESSON

Summarize and Evaluate

Gather the class together. Spend some time reviewing. Use newsprint or chalkboard to make a list and thus help the students retain their new learning.

Closing

Sing the theme song "We Are the Children of God." Thank the class for their cooperation and help during the lesson.

✳ TEACHING TIP ✳

Acceptable behavior is one way we sometimes promote inappropriate gender stereotyping. If we allow boys to be more rambunctious in class because "that's the way they are," yet admonish girls for similar activity because "it's not lady-like," we are sending strong messages.

Boys play differently from girls and may behave in very different ways publicly. However, try not to excuse boys from established class behavior. Try not to promote a double standard for boys' behavior and girls' behavior.

Also don't compare the genders. If a standard behavior has been set, and someone is not acting within that standard, the consequences should be consistent. The same should go for the standard of work, study, reading, and class participation. It may be difficult to maintain a consistent standard, but it sends a strong positive message. You are saying that boys and girls are subject to the same rules in the same way—no exceptions.

PARENT TAKE-HOME SHEET

Lesson 8: Media and Stereotypes

In Today's Lesson

We talked about how the media shape our stereotypes. Through television shows, movies, radio programs, and the print media including books and advertising, we are being shaped to think about gender characteristics that are not true. These patterns put women and men down.

Discussion Questions

Discover as a family how the media feed us lies about what men do and what women do. Ask yourself and other adults these questions:

- Why is it okay to advertise feminine hygiene products, but not masculine hygiene products?

- How many news stories on medical conditions related to women have you heard compared to the number related to men? An example would be to note the number of times that breast cancer makes the news versus the frequency that prostate cancer is reviewed.

- Why does teen pregnancy so often focus on the woman, not the man? Pregnancy is seen as the woman's problem and seldom reviewed as equally the man's responsibility.

- Why do shapely women in bikinis often appear in beer ads?

- In some commercials, such as mouthwash commercials, insecticide commercials, and some car commercials, there are no human beings, or there are babies with no gender identified. What gender do you assume for the nonhuman objects in these ads? Why?

- How many times do men on TV and in movies rescue women? How often are women portrayed as naïve, but men are streetwise?

Ask to see the forms your children worked with this week. The forms help them look critically at the messages being transmitted in our world through various media.

You are encouraged to regard the media with a critical eye and ear. Suggest doing this with a group of your friends. The incessant messages affect the way we look at the world. We believe what the media tell us, and there is more and more evidence that we are trying to live up to what we are told.

Family Activity

Look at your favorite TV show, and talk about the messages each person saw or heard that relate to gender issues. Are these messages true or false?

Rent a video that you have already watched, and assign one character to one or two people. Ask them to observe whether the person is behaving the way we expect a woman or man to act. Does the person's behavior reflect what happens in real life? Use the forms that your children used during class to help you. Ask the class leaders for copies if they did not include them with this take-home sheet.

Parent Tip

Sit with your children during their favorite TV show. Learn about the gender and other messages being given. In cartoon shows, women are often in distress and wear tight clothes. The heroes are usually men who are loners and commit violence without emotional attachment.

Nonanimated shows may also send negative messages. Some are subtle and may need a parental eye. Ask your children what they like about the show. Ask them about the main characters. What would they be like if they were real people? Do the people they know act like the people on TV? Do they learn something from watching the show?

It is not always necessary or even desirable to put down a show that your children watch. Try to encourage them to be critical about the examples and information they receive from watching a TV show. Then give your own favorite show the same critical analysis. Better yet, ask your children to help you!

Next Lesson

We will talk about Queen Vashti in the book of Esther. We will discuss why she said no to the king's request.

TELEVISION ACTIVITY PAGE

Commercials

What product is being sold?

Which gender is more prominent?

In what capacity are people portrayed?

Are the men dressed differently from the women?

What roles does each gender play?

What hidden message is conveyed about women? About men?

Are only faces shown, or are body parts viewed as well? Why?

If animation is used, are the objects assumed to be male or female?

TV Shows

Is the main character male or female?

Which gender of character seems to be a leader, and which is a follower?

Do men make sexual comments about women? How many?

Do women make sexual comments about men? How many?

Do men "rescue" women from situations?

Are women the chief nurturers?

Are women dressed provocatively, showing lots of leg, midriff, navel, or cleavage?

Are men dressed provocatively?

Does either gender pose provocatively? Who? When? Why?

What would you conclude about women from what you saw?

What would you conclude about men?

Sexual Harassment

Biblical Text: Esther 1 (story of Queen Vashti, paraphrased)
Focus: Sexual harassment is a reality in our society. Women and sometimes even men are forced by threats and intimidation to do what they think is wrong. The focus of this lesson is to help children understand and confront the reality of sexual harassment.
Bible Memory: Psalm 28:6–9

Bible Story (told by Queen Vashti in her older years)

Long ago, everyone in this great kingdom probably thought that I was the luckiest woman of all to be married to the king! How lucky I was to enjoy his wealth and riches and to be so beautiful! The people did not know how difficult my life was.

My husband, King Ahasuerus, ruled from India to Ethiopia, 127 provinces. He commanded a great army, and he was very rich. He was also a big show-off. He enjoyed bragging about how much land he ruled and how large his army was.

The king gave a party for all the men who lived in the capital city of Susa. It was held in the garden court of the royal pavilion and lasted for seven days. There were white curtains and violet hangings fastened to silver rings with bands of fine linen and purple; there were alabaster pillars and couches of gold and silver set on a mosaic pavement of malachite and alabaster, mother-of-pearl and turquoise. The king displayed jewels, expensive dishes, and furniture for all the men to see. The king served the men fine food, and wine was served in golden cups. He ordered the servants and slaves to give each man as much wine as he wished.

At the same time that the king had a party, I had a party for the women in the royal apartments of the king.

By the seventh day of the party, the king had drunk a lot of wine; in fact, he was drunk. In this drunken state he demanded that I make an appearance so that he could show all the men of Susa how beautiful I was. I was glad that the king thought I was beautiful, but I did not think that it was a good idea for me to obey the king and go to his party. The rumor was that he was going to ask me to parade before the men wearing only my royal crown.

At first I did not know what to do. I knew that the queen was always expected to follow the orders of the king. I knew that most of the people in the land would think that it was bad to refuse an order of the king.

I was also afraid. I was afraid of the drunken men and the king. I was afraid of what the king might do if I refused to follow his command. But in my heart I knew that it was wrong for me to go to his party.

I was also angry. I did not want to do what he said this time. He had no right to order me to display my beauty to the men.

So I refused to go to the party. The king was so angry that he didn't know what to do. He gathered together the princes of Persia and other wise men to ask them what he should do because I had refused his order. They convinced the king that I had done wrong to the king, to the officers, and to all the people in the kingdom. The advisors said that soon every woman in the kingdom would have heard about my refusal and all the women would treat their husbands with contempt. The women would refuse their husbands' demands, and there would be endless disrespect and insolence!

The king decided to issue a royal decree to be read throughout the land. It said that I would never be allowed to appear before the king again and I would lose my place as queen. Another queen would be selected.

The king also sent letters to all the royal provinces to say that all women would give honor to their husbands. He declared that each man was the master of his own house and he could control all the women in the home.

Well, it wasn't long until Esther was chosen to be queen. I never saw the king again. I was sorry that the king had sent out that edict. It wasn't fair and it wasn't right. People should not be forced to do what they think is wrong. Women should not be forced to parade themselves for the pleasure of others. No one should be forced to kiss or hug someone. I think I did the right thing when I refused to go to the king at that drunken party.

Theological/Biblical Perspective

The book of Esther begins with a banquet held by the Persian king Ahasuerus for all the men who live in the capital city of Susa. At this banquet after much wild drinking, the king summons Queen Vashti. He demands her appearance before the court so that he can show off her great beauty. While he characterizes the queen's refusal to appear as a lack of obedience to his demand, the men of the kingdom view this refusal even more seriously. They see it as a threat to the dominance of every husband. Therefore, the king banishes her from the court.

The text does not tell us why Queen Vashti refused to appear. The Aramaic translation of the Hebrew Scriptures informs the readers that the king wished Queen Vashti to appear naked before the company and that out of modesty she refused. Whatever her reason for refusing to appear before the drunken court of men, Queen Vashti can certainly be characterized as a strong female character who lost her position because of her refusal to appear as the king demanded. She chose the right action against the king's demand.

Too often in our society, people are forced to comply with demands that they know are wrong. Historically women, in particular, have been forced into sexual activity at the demands of others. Today we understand that this forced activity is wrong, and it is called sexual harassment.

Children need to learn to resist pressure and demands from others to do what is wrong. In addition, they need to understand the importance of not participating in such pressure or coercion. Middle schools and junior high schools are filled with sexual teasing and pressure. Unfortunately, churches are not always free from sexual harassment. Therefore, we would do well to teach children in church about gender discrimination and sexual harassment.

Anticipated Outcomes

- ◆ To learn the story of Queen Vashti.
- ◆ To explore the concept of gender discrimination and sexual harassment.
- ◆ To understand some of the consequences of discrimination.

Resources Needed

All Grades:
  ◆ Costume for Queen Vashti

Grades K–2:
  ◆ Poster board (one board per two children in the class)
  ◆ Markers, pencils, crayons

Grades 3–5:
  ◆ Footprints

Grades 6–8:
  ◆ Roll of paper (10″ to 12″ high)
  ◆ Wooden rods for ends of scrolls

  ◆ Markers

Teacher Preparation

1. This lesson includes the story of Queen Vashti. This is a wonderful story to be told in first person. Either study the story yourself or ask someone in your church to appear before the class as Queen Vashti many years after her banishment. Dress in a costume. You may want to encourage the children to ask questions about what happened.

(Grades 3–5) 2. Inside the footprints included in this lesson are facts about men and women from history. Photocopy these pages, and cut out the footprints.

(Grades 6–8) 3. Make scrolls for groups of three or four children. The students will write their own decrees on the scrolls.

4. At any time during these sessions, a child may disclose that harassment or abuse has taken place in his or her life. Think ahead about how

you may respond if a child trusts you and/or the class to tell this secret. Know the local child protective service number.

Consider these points:

- Be sure that the pastor knows the theme of this lesson. Contact him or her immediately after any disclosure of sexual abuse or harassment.
- Listen carefully and be supportive as the child tells about his or her experience.
- Tell the child that you believe he or she is telling the truth. Reassure the child that what has happened is not his or her fault.
- Thank the child for sharing with you, and make it clear that you are very sorry that this has happened to him or her.
- Explain that you will do everything you can to make the abuse or harassment stop. In order to help the child, you must tell other people who can help.

Above all, reassure the child that you will continue to be supportive.

GETTING STARTED

Gather the class together. Explain that for today's lesson, you will have a special guest coming to tell the class about her experience a long time ago. Introduce Queen Vashti to the class.

DEVELOPING THE LESSON

Divide the class into three broad age groups. The discussions that develop may not be appropriate for everyone to hear.

Ask Queen Vashti to tell her story. (See "Bible Story.")

Lead the class in the appropriate discussion:

Grades K–2:

- Is this really Queen Vashti visiting our classroom?
- How do you think Queen Vashti felt when the king asked her to come to the party?
- Why did Queen Vashti refuse?
- Have you ever felt that someone asked you to do something wrong?
- What does God want you to do when you are asked to do something wrong?

Grades 3–5:

- Review the story of Queen Vashti with the class (see discussion questions with younger children).
- Did Queen Vashti have the right to refuse to go to the party?

Grades 6–8:

- Review the story of Queen Vashti with the class (see discussion questions with younger children).
- What do you think about King Ahasuerus's edicts and decrees?
- How do you think that the people of the kingdom felt about Queen Vashti?
- Would the women have felt differently from the way the men did?
- Have attitudes changed since Queen Vashti's time? How?
- List things that are wrong that someone might try to force you to do (for example, take drugs, kiss someone, steal something, etc.).
- What can you do if someone tries to force or trick you to do something wrong?

All groups: Ask the students if they know the definition of sexual harassment. Explain that sexual harassment occurs when someone makes sexual comments or jokes; tries to do something sexual, such as kiss you or hug you; bothers you by touching you in your private parts; or pressures you to touch him or her on the private parts. The person may continue this behavior even when you have told him or her to stop.

Remind the children that the best thing to do is to tell a grown-up about what is happening to them. Tell parents, a teacher, the pastor, or someone else. These adults will help you feel safe.

Response Activities

Grades 6–8: Write New Edicts and Decrees

Remind the class that King Ahasuerus sent out decrees and edicts to all the provinces. These edicts said that wives must honor their husbands and obey every command.

Divide the class into small groups of three or four. Include both boys and girls in each group.

Encourage the groups to write new edicts and decrees that are fair for both men and women, boys and girls.

Ask each group to choose one person to read the edicts.

Invite all groups to explain why the edicts are fair.

All Grades: The Footprints Game

Shuffle the cutout footprints, and pass them out among the class members. Direct the students to stand in a line, side by side. After each child reads his or her footprint, decide together how many steps forward or backward this person should take, depending on how positive or negative the class views that footprint fact. Continue to do this until all the footprints have been read.

Encourage class members to add true stories about the changing roles of men and women, boys and girls.

Grades K–2: Make a Poster

Ask the children to form groups of two or three. Explain that they are to make posters reminding children that they can say no when someone asks them to do something wrong. For example, they could draw a picture of Queen Vashti telling the messenger that she will not dance for the king.

Brainstorm about other things that they could put on the posters.

Give each group markers, crayons, pencils, and poster board.

When each group is finished, ask the groups to share their posters.

Optional Activity

A Story of a Queen in Our Time

Depending on the size of the class, the class can be divided into smaller groups, or the entire group can work as a whole. Rewrite the story of Queen Vashti for our time.

In the modern story, the character of Queen Vashti could be any woman. Remember that in some cases men have been sexually harassed too. Sexual harassment occurs when someone exerts force or pressures someone else into doing something sexual that he or she doesn't want to do. Oftentimes the person exerting the pressure won't stop—even when asked to stop.

Write the story so that it is similar to the biblical story.

Ask each group to read its version, and discuss the different versions that the class created.

CONCLUDING THE LESSON

Summarize and Evaluate

Gather the class together. Ask the class, "If you were telling someone about this lesson, what would you say?" Review the major concepts of the lesson. Invite anyone who wants to talk more about the lesson today to stay after class or contact the teacher in another way.

Closing

Read Psalm 28:6–9.

Explain to the class that no matter what happens to us, God is with us. God is always there. God is a source of comfort and strength to help us through the challenges of life.

Close the class with a prayer: "Dear God, we ask that you continue to be with each of us. Sometimes people ask us to do things that we know are wrong. Give us strength to say no. Give us courage to tell others when we have been wronged. Amen."

✳ TEACHING TIP ✳

The children may have difficult questions about sexual harassment in this lesson. Particularly older children will want to know more because of their own experience. Recent studies in junior high schools revealed that the experience of being sexually harassed is common. Many girls and boys experience being teased in school about sex. They are often forced to listen to sexual jokes that are demeaning and insulting. They often aren't sure whom they can tell about their experience, and many of them believe that it is a situation they have to learn to live with.

It is important, as a trusted adult in these children's lives, that you are willing to listen. During the closing moments of this class, it is recommended that you make yourself available to any student who wants to talk about his or her personal experience. Listen carefully. You may need to go with the child to talk to his or her parents, or you may want to suggest the involvement of a school counselor or administrator.

For more information, see *Preventing Child Sexual Abuse: A Curriculum for Children Ages 9–12* by Kathryn Goering Reid with Marie M. Fortune (Cleveland: United Church Press, 1989).

PARENT TAKE-HOME SHEET

Lesson 9: Sexual Harassment

In Today's Lesson
We learned the story of Queen Vashti and how she refused to do what she thought was wrong.

We discussed the concept of discrimination.

We identified some ways we may have an impact on the reduction of discrimination in our world.

Discussion Questions

Describe experiences in which you feel that you were pressured or tricked into doing something you considered wrong.

- What did you do?
- How did you feel?
- Which persons did you tell?

Family Activity

No matter how alone we feel, we can always tell God about our feelings. Our communication with God takes place individually and communally. We pray alone, and we pray with others. We pray in church and with our families.

Here is another way to communicate with God: write a letter. The letter doesn't go through the mail, but in writing words on the page, we give those thoughts and words to God, just as we do in prayer.

As a family, compose a letter to God. Tell God how you feel.

Dear God,

_____

_____

_____

_____

_____

_____

_____

_____

_____

_____

_____

Love,

_____

Parent Tip

One of the greatest challenges facing parents is teaching children to respect authority and at the same time not blindly follow authority. We want to teach our children to say no to drugs and other harmful substances. We don't want them to question rules that are important for their safety and welfare.

Although the majority of persons in authority are kind and caring, some powerful people use threats and intimidation to make others who are weaker do things that are wrong. As parents, we must rely on balance in teaching our children. We must teach them to listen carefully to the guidance of those in authority, yet understand that there may be times when they must say no to someone because they are asked to do something wrong.

Next Lesson

Our last lesson in this curriculum will tie it all together and help us review all the material that we have had in the last quarter.

THE FOOTPRINTS GAME

Free to Be...You and Me is a book, record, and play created in 1972. It included a song to tell boys they could cry and a story to tell boys they could have dolls. Was Free to Be...You and Me a step forward or backward?

Women today spend more time doing housework than in the 1920s. Families change their clothes more often and expect a cleaner house and more exciting meals. Is this a step forward or backward?

When your parents were born, husbands waited alone in a room to be told whether their wives had a baby boy or girl. Your grandfather did not get to see his children being born. Is this a step forward or backward?

In Bible times, Hebrew boys attended school at the synagogue while girls stayed home and helped their mothers with the housework. Was that a step forward or backward from the way things are today?

In Jesus' time, men were not allowed to talk to women in public. Jesus broke this rule and spoke to women in the street. Did Jesus take us a step forward or backward?

In Bible times when a girl was old enough to marry, her parents had to give the future husband gifts or money called a dowry. If a woman's family was poor, the dowry would be small, and it would be hard to find the daughter a husband. Was that a step forward or backward from today?

In Bible times, men worshiped in one room in the Temple while the women and children had to be silent in a separate room. At twelve years of age, boys had a ceremony to mark the time when they could join the men in their room. Was that a step forward or backward from today?

On January 15, 1911, Anna J. Allebach was ordained a minister of the General Conference of Mennonite churches at First Mennonite Church in Philadelphia. Her ministry included preaching, teaching, and helping people. She became the pastor of Sunnyside Reformed Church, Long Island. Although she occasionally preached in Mennonite churches, she never received a call to be a pastor of a church in her own denomination. Was that a step forward or backward at that time?

In fairy stories a dragon or a wicked person captures a princess. Later a brave prince rescues and marries her. *The Paper Bag Princess* is a story by Robert Munsch that has a brave princess rescue a prince from a dragon. She decides not to marry him. Has Robert Munsch taken us a step forward or backward?

Mattie Dolby and her brother Joe were the first black students at Manchester College, a Church of the Brethren college in Indiana. Although they were allowed to attend college, they were forced to cook their meals off campus, away from other students. Did Mattie and Joe take us a step forward or backward?

In 1993 the Texas State Department of Education ruled that all public school systems must allow girls who are qualified to play on school football teams with boys. The department reasoned that since there are no girls' football teams, girls must be allowed to play. The Department of Education said that it was only fair. Was that a step forward or backward?

In December 1946, Selma Pratt, a member of the Bethel College Mennonite Church, helped to organize the Newton Interracial Fellowship. One of the activities of this group was to work toward integration of movie theaters, restaurants, and drugstore soda fountains in Newton, Kansas. This organization also helped to foster mutual understanding among people with varied racial and ethnic backgrounds. Was that a step forward or backward?

You Are Chosen!

Biblical Texts:

Joshua 4:1–9 (Joshua and the people cross the Jordan)

Matthew 28:16–20 (the Great Commission)

Luke 24:44–53 (the ascension of Christ)

Focus: This lesson is a combination of celebration and affirmation of what we have accomplished in the preceding lessons. We want to see how the children apply some of the things they have learned. This week we will help them to remember some of what they have learned and give them a chance to use their creativity to confront and change some of the gender stereotypes that distort our world. We want to send them out with a sense of what God wills for all humankind—to grow, work, play, lead, teach, and learn together. The participants have been through an intensive ten weeks. But we hope that this will not be the end of their experience. During this time, we want the students to experience once again the opportunities of cooperative work.

Bible Memory: Genesis 1:27

Theological/Biblical Perspective

Today we want to focus on some of the most famous future-oriented passages. We see the time when Joshua made sure that God's faithfulness would be told to future generations. Similarly, Christ prepared the disciples for what was ahead of them with the Great Commission and his ascension.

God will continue to empower us, just as the disciples were empowered after they experienced the true way. It was their experience of Jesus' teachings plus the continued encouragement and opportunity to put into practice what they had learned that gave them the impetus to begin a new church. Doing by teaching and practice is a model we must make our own in order to plant real seeds of change.

Anticipated Outcomes

- That children will discover that God wants to empower them to continue what they have learned during these lessons.
- That they will practice solutions to confront some of the injustices they will encounter.
- That they will remember that girls and boys should never be judged by gender.

Resources Needed

All Grades:

- Two 3-inch squares of contrasting colored paper for each child (red and green if available)
- Chalkboard and chalk, or newsprint and markers
- Newsprint, markers, and drawing paper

Grades 6–8:

- Set of chairs (see game suggestion about obstacles to equality)

Make a large Tic-Tac-Toe game on a large sheet of newsprint. Make five squares with "X" and five squares with "O" on them to use for the game.

Teacher Preparation

1. Set up the chalkboard or newsprint to record the answers for the opening session.

2. Set up the chairs for the junior youth game.

GETTING STARTED

Greet each child and hand out the paper described in the opening exercise.

Tell the children that the class will end a little earlier than usual because there is something special for them to do.

Opening Exercise

Give each child a green square of paper and a red square of paper (or any two contrasting colors). They can be about 3 inches square.

Read Joshua 4:1–9. Read the statements and tell the children to hold up a green card if the statement is true or a red card if it is false.

1. Joshua meant to pick up only the stones from the middle of the river.

2. He chose men because women were too weak to pick up the stones.

3. He chose men because men usually represented their tribe.

4. Joshua told the men to place the stones in a pile.

5. The stones were to remind the people about how faithful God was.

6. Only boys could ask what the stones meant.

Ask one person to be Joshua and role-play choosing persons from the total class to pick up the stones, realizing that this would have been a very great honor. Would Joshua have chosen women and men if he were around today? What if Miriam, Moses' sister, had chosen twelve people? Whom would she have chosen, and why?

Read the Great Commission. Repeat the same true or false process with these statements.

1. Jesus spoke only to the male disciples.

2. There were no women disciples.

3. Women didn't play a very important part in Jesus' ministry.

4. Jesus did not want women to teach.

5. Jesus wanted the people listening to make disciples.

6. The women could teach, but not baptize.

Not everything that Jesus said was recorded. What else could Jesus have said if this class was there when he gave the Great Commission? What would Jesus have said about being fair to both boys and girls? What would he have told the class to do?

DEVELOPING THE LESSON

Below is a story to read to the children.

Grades K–2 and Grades 3–5 Activity

Read the story for the children, then divide them into groupings of young children and middle graders for the activities that follow the story.

IN THE PLAYGROUND

Hi, I'm Jenny. Jeffrey and I are best friends. We do our best talking in the playground. Sometimes we just hang on the monkey bars and talk. We talk about all kinds of things. Jeffrey wants to be a dancer when he grows up. I want to be a firefighter.

John and Larry, two sixth graders, came by yesterday.

"What are you doing talking to a girl?" asked Larry.

Jeffrey said, "This is Jenny. She and I are best friends."

John laughed, "You can't have a girl for a best friend, unless you want to marry her."

"That's not true," said Jeffrey.

"It is," said John, "and everybody knows it. And girls can't hang on the monkey bars as good as boys because boys are stronger."

"I can hang on the bars for fifteen minutes," I said to John. "And I can hang upside down and count to a hundred without getting a headache or throwing up or anything."

Larry said, "I can hang upside down and count to a million." I knew Larry couldn't do it, but I didn't say anything.

Larry asked Jeffrey, "Want to play football?"

"Nah," said Jeffrey, "I don't like playing football."

"I'll play," I said

John said, "You're a girl. Girls aren't smart enough to play football."

"You don't have to be smart," said Jeffrey. "You have to be quick and a good runner. Well, Jenny is quick and a good runner and strong and smart."

"I want to be a firefighter when I grow up," I said.

"That's dumb. Girls can't be firefighters." Both John and Larry laughed.

"Girls can be anything they want. So can boys," I said. "Jeffrey wants to be a dancer."

Larry said, "Jeffrey, that's funny, there are no men dancers."

"There are too," said Jeffrey. "What about Baryshnikov and Nureyev and Fred Astaire?"

John said, "You're making those names up. Boys can't be dancers and everyone knows it."

Larry and John walked away laughing. We didn't say anything for a while. Then I said, "Jeffrey, when you become a dancer, I will come to all your performances and shout hurray."

Jeffrey said, "And if there is ever a fire, I will call you so you can save me and my cat."

Grades K–2 Activity

Position two large pieces of paper on the wall. Invite the children to think about ways boys and girls are different. List them on one piece of paper. Then invite them to think about ways boys and girls are the same. List them on the other piece. Next encourage the children to draw a picture about Jenny and Jeffrey playing something together. Leave enough wall space between the two lists to exhibit these drawings.

Grades 3–5 Activity

Gather in teams of two to four people, and ask them to consider what they would do in the following situations:

- You see a girl surrounded by boys who are shouting at her. One boy pushes her down, and they all laugh at her.

- You want to join a soccer team that has boys and girls playing on it. You find out that they will not let you on the team because they have enough boys (or girls) on the team already.

- You see a boy hurt himself when he is playing with other boys. They make fun of him when he starts crying. They call him names and won't let him play anymore.

- There is a new girl in school but no one will talk to her because she is "different." She always stands by herself, watching the others play. The other girls always make terrible jokes about her.

Tell the teams to role-play what they would do in each situation. Or each team may pick one situation and role-play it for the others, then explain why the team responded as it did.

Grades 6–8 Activity

Divide the group into two teams. If possible, maintain gender balance between the teams. Give each team its own set of brightly colored squares and place the large Tic-Tac-Toe newsprint sheet on the floor. Teams are to alternate in responding to the questions and situations provided below. In each case, they are asked to pretend they can speak or act the way they would really like. After responding, the team puts a marker in an empty space on the Tic-Tac-Toe sheet. If a team passes on a question, they forfeit their turn. Otherwise, the rules are the same as for Tic-Tac-Toe.

1. In the playground someone says to you, "Boys always have to play the superhero because they do in the movies and on TV. Girls are always the ones who get saved from danger because they can't do it themselves." What would you say or do?

2. You are a teacher. You hear another teacher say, "Girls are not good at physics, chemistry, technical drawing, or computers. Boys are not good at poetry, cooking, languages, or art." What would you say or do?

3. During quiz time, the teacher picks more boys than girls, even though everyone puts their hand up. What would you say or do?

4. Someone says, "Girls are supposed to cry when they hurt themselves. Boys are never supposed to cry, unless they're sissies and wusses." What would you say or do?

5. Most of the books you use in class include stories and pictures related to sports to help explain difficult math and science subjects. Is that OK?

6. In class a girl misbehaves and the teacher says, "You should know better than that. That is not the way young ladies behave." A boy misbehaves and the teacher says, "Now, now, enough fooling around. We all know how funny you are. Let's get back to work." What would you say or do?

7. A friend of yours says, "I never go to watch girls' sports teams. Boys' sports are faster and more exciting." What would you say or do?

8. Whenever a boy answers a question in class, the teacher always asks him another question and they have a mini-discussion. Whenever a girl

answers a question, the teacher responds simply and moves on. What would you say or do?

9. In sports, a boys' team is playing against a girls' team. You hear an adult say, "If the girls beat the boys, that's bad. If the boys beat the girls, so what? It's only a girls team." What would you say or do?

CONCLUDING THE LESSON

Summarize and Evaluate

Gather the group together. Think about some of the important words that you remember from this series of lessons, such as "love," "God," "all people," and "fairness."

Ask if anyone in the group knows how to sign these words. If the class is lucky enough to have someone who can sign, encourage that student to teach the rest of the class.

If no one can sign, invite the group to think of motions or actions that would communicate each word.

Closing

Thank the children for participating in this series of lessons. Remind them that they do not always have to pray with their eyes closed. The prayer to close this lesson will concern doing the motions you just learned. In a prayerlike spirit, lead the class through the motions. Close the prayer with an "amen."

PARENT TAKE-HOME SHEET

Lesson 10: You Are Chosen!

In Today's Lesson

We discovered that God wants to empower us to continue what we have learned during these lessons.

We learned that we can find solutions to confront some of the injustices based on gender.

We discovered that girls and boys should never be judged by gender, but should be recognized as unique and wonderful.

An Open Letter to Parents

We, the writers of this curriculum, want to thank you for being supportive during these ten weeks. Your children have learned a lot and have probably thought about a lot of things for the first time. Some of the issues and examples covered in this series may not be familiar to you or to your children. Nevertheless, they are real and are a part of our world. We hope that this curriculum has been a source of hope as well as a resource for problem solving and a celebration of God's intention that we all live in God's fullness as human beings not bound by stereotypes.

We realize that much of the work in bringing up children rests with people like you. We also realize that, as primary caregivers, you have a lot to think about and be responsible for. We want to thank you again for the work you have done and wish you God's richest blessings as you travel with your children into the future. Our hope is that your care and concern to overcome intolerance in our world will make a difference for everyone's children. It happens one person at a time.

There is no take-home sheet this week. We ask that you review with your children the sheets from the previous weeks and continue to think of ways you can help break down gender, racial, and other intolerance and stereotypes.

Contact us if you have any questions. You are not alone. Together we can be a voice to usher in a new world, as God intended. You can reach us both in care of United Church Press, 700 Prospect Ave., Cleveland, OH 44115.

Shalom,

Kathy Goering Reid
Ken Hawkley